趣味識字
Fun with Chinese
A Chinese Character Learning Curriculum

第十六冊
Workbook 16

自序

我是一位在美國的自學媽媽,孩子的中文學習完全由我親自教導。

在傳統教學方式的薰陶下許多家長認為孩子學中文必須先從注音開始,往往也認為中文字筆畫眾多複雜對小孩來說太難。其實對幼兒來說每一個中文字都只是一個圖案,幼兒的記憶力非常強,認字對他們來說並不困難。

我自己的兩個孩子都是從認字開始學習中文的。當初我會設計趣味識字是因為在市面上並沒有找到令我完全滿意的教材,絕大多數的教材都是從注音符號或是筆畫簡單的字開始教學。雖然筆劃較少容易書寫但往往這些字在日常生活上並不常見,在孩子的世界裡更是沒有應用的機會。而市面上認字的教材卻普遍地缺乏動手的參與感。孩子在學習的過程中常常覺得教材枯燥乏味,既沒趣味又缺乏實用性。這樣的學習對孩子來說不但痛苦也沒有效率。使用這些教材後我發現自己一直在動手製作輔助教材來提昇孩子的學習興趣。

我一直深信一定要讓孩子覺得有趣和實用,他們才會有學習的動力,有了動力才會學得好。所以趣味識字的設計是以先教常用字的方式讓孩子能夠快速進入閱讀,因而發覺識字的實用性。當孩子懂得如何應用文字後,學習自信自然就提高了。製作輔助教材時為了幫助孩子加強對生字的記憶,除了使用字卡和遊戲的方式複習,我也設計了一系列的遊戲習題,而這些習題就是趣味識字誕生的前奏。

最後非常感謝您選擇趣味識字做為孩子的教材,也希望這套教材可以幫助您的孩子快樂學習中文。

Preface

I am a homeschooling mom in America who successfully taught my two children to read Chinese at a young age.

Many people think that learning Chinese must start with pinyin because Chinese characters are too complicated and believed to be too difficult for children. However, in children's minds, each Chinese character is just like a picture and memorization is not difficult for them.

Both my children learned to read Chinese beginning with character recognition, yet the process was not easy for me. Existing textbooks often start teaching with pinyin or start with rarely used characters with minimal strokes for writing. Books that emphasize character recognition also tend to be less interactive and less hands-on causing the learning process to be tedious and unmotivating for children. I found myself constantly needing to create my own teaching materials while using these textbooks; and this is the reason for the creation of Fun with Chinese.

Fun with Chinese is designed to teach the most commonly used Chinese characters first, quickly allowing children to be able to read meaningful phrases and sentences from the very beginning. Pictures and games are also used to help with character retention, and each lesson includes reading passages to review previously learned characters.

Today, I am sharing with you this wonderful system that I have used with my own children and hoping to make your child's Chinese learning an easy and enjoyable journey.

— Anchia Tai

關於英文翻譯

習題本中的句子都有中英雙語,希望讓中文不是很好的家長們也有辦法使用教材。其中朗讀句子練習中的英文翻譯也盡量讓句型和中文相對應幫助英文為母語的家長容易理解。

About the English Translations

The English translations in the workbooks are specifically designed in a way to closely match up with the Chinese sentence grammar structure. While this might make the translations grammatically incorrect in English, the design will help English speakers to learn and understand the Chinese sentences better.

關於筆順

本書中的國字筆順是依據中華民國教育部「常用國字標準字體筆順學習網」的筆劃順序彙編。中華民國教育部對於部分筆順有做調整,可能於傳統書寫筆順有所差異,不同華人地區的筆順也可能有所不同。如果本書中的筆順與家長所學的筆順有所差異,請自行調整教學。

About the Stroke Orders

The stroke orders of the characters in this workbook follow the stroke orders provided on the "Learning Program for Stroke Order of Frequently Used Chinese Characters" website of the Ministry of Education, R.O.C. (Taiwan). The authors are aware that there were changes to the stroke orders made by the Ministry of Education as well as regional differences in character stroke orders. Please feel free to make adjustments in teaching if the stroke orders are different in your region.

每當完成一課後請回到本頁將該課的吊鐘塗上顏色。
Please color a bell after you have completed a lesson.

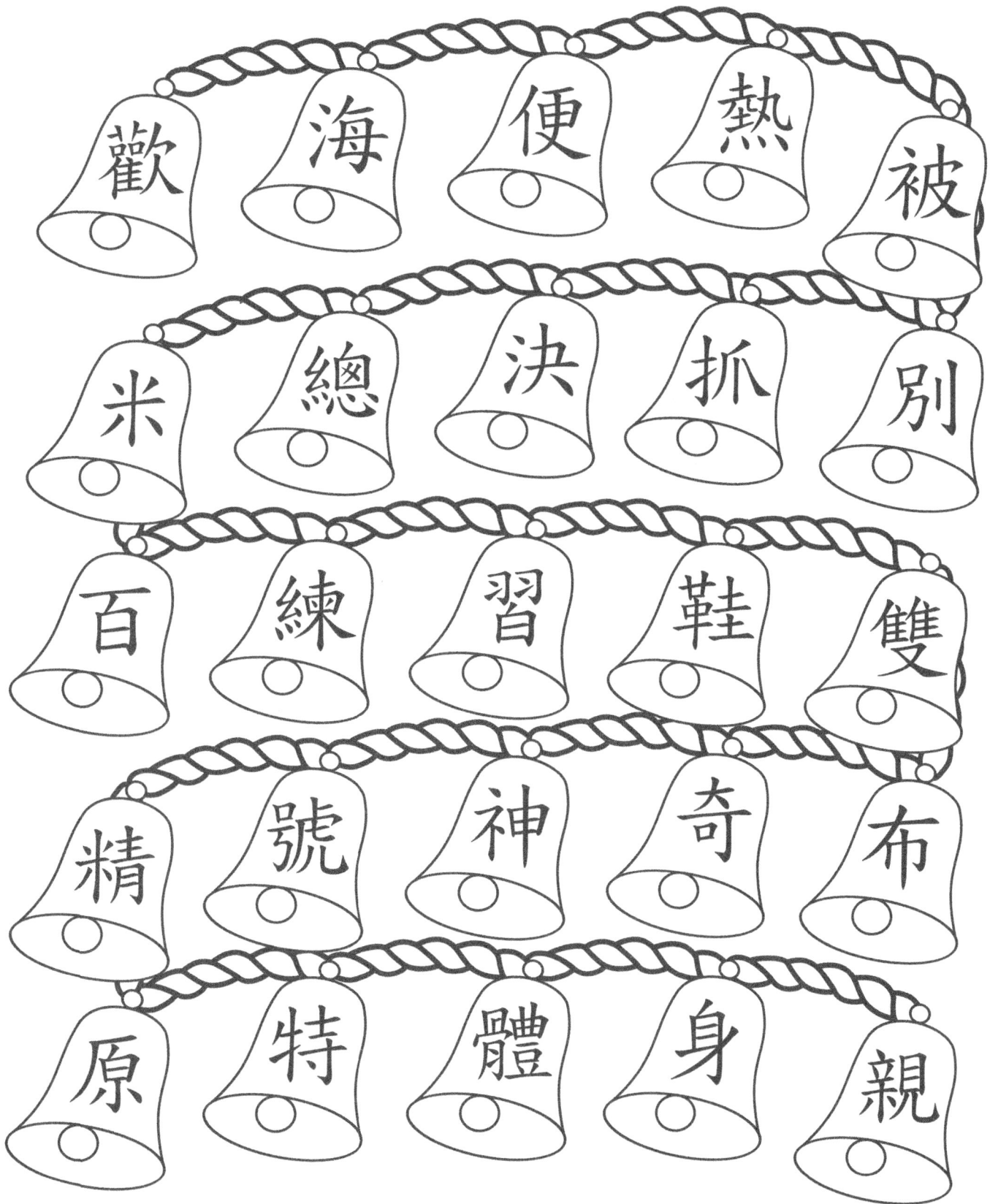

第一課
Lesson 1 Huān – joyous; happy; pleased

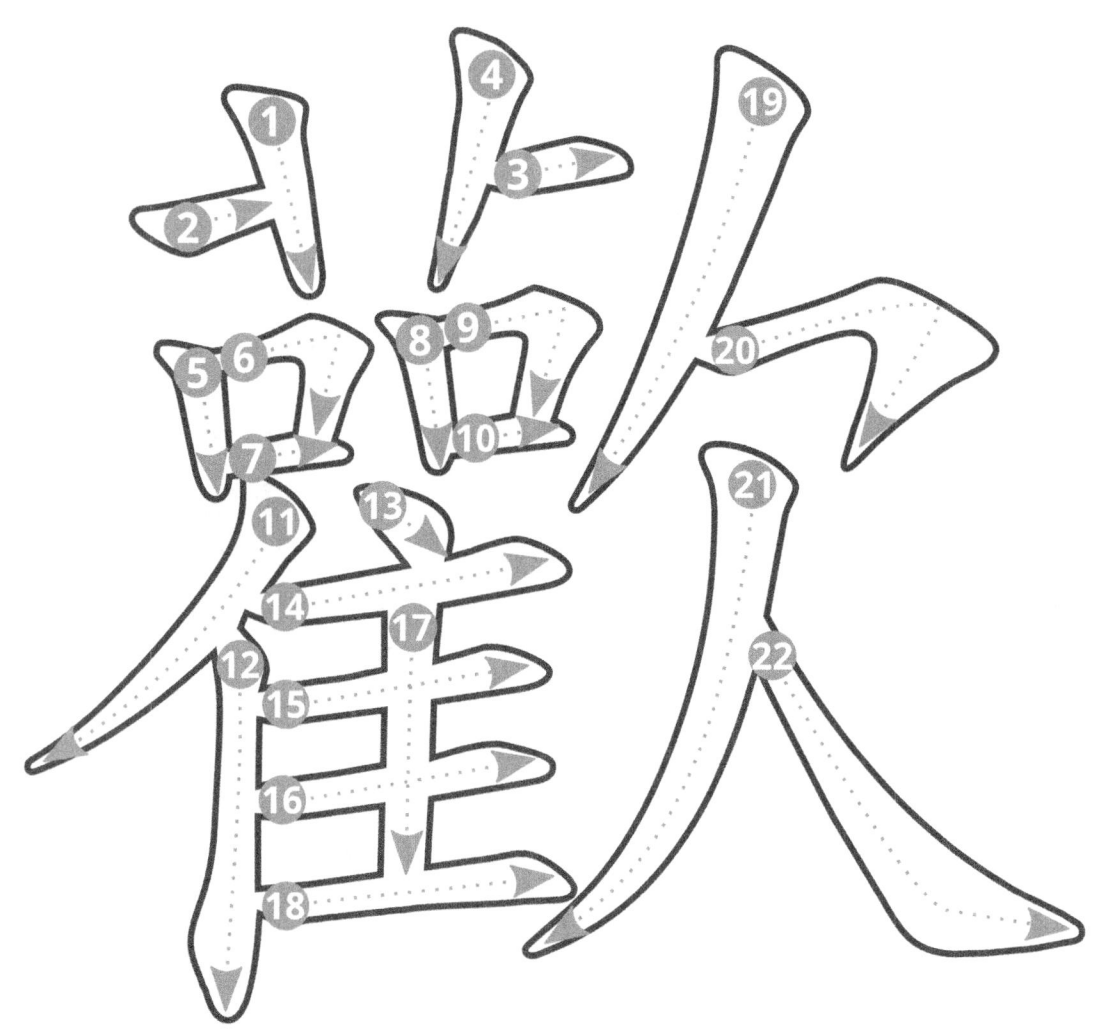

本書中的國字筆順是依據中華民國教育部「常用國字標準字體筆順學習網」的筆劃順序彙編。
The stroke orders of the characters in this workbook follow the stroke orders provided on the "Learning Program for Stroke Order of Frequently Used Chinese Characters" website of the Ministry of Education, R.O.C. (Taiwan).

閱讀測驗。請在正確答案的前面打勾。
Read the following paragraph and answer the questions below.

我喜歡打球、小美喜歡畫畫、小麗喜歡唱歌。小明什麼都不喜歡，只喜歡在家裡睡覺。

1. 誰喜歡唱歌？
   ( ) 小明
   ( ) 小麗
   ( ) 我
2. 下面哪個是對的？
   ( ) 我喜歡畫畫
   ( ) 小明喜歡唱歌
   ( ) 小明喜歡睡覺

唸出下面的語詞。
Read aloud the phrases below.

唸唸看
Read-Aloud

- 我喜歡做加法的題目。
  I like to do addition problems.

- 妹妹比較喜歡學中文。
  (My) younger sister likes to learn Chinese more.

- 媽媽讓我教妹妹數學。
  Mom lets me teach (my) younger sister math.

- 妹妹覺得加法很難。
  (My) younger sister thinks addition is very difficult.

- 如果用小石頭來算也許妹妹就不會覺得難了。
  If (she) uses little pebbles to count, maybe (my) younger sister won't think (it) is difficult.

恭喜你完成了這一課,請回到第一頁將本課的吊鐘塗上顏色。
Congratulations! You have completed a lesson. Please color the bell for this lesson on page 1.

第二課

Lesson 2 Hǎi – ocean; sea

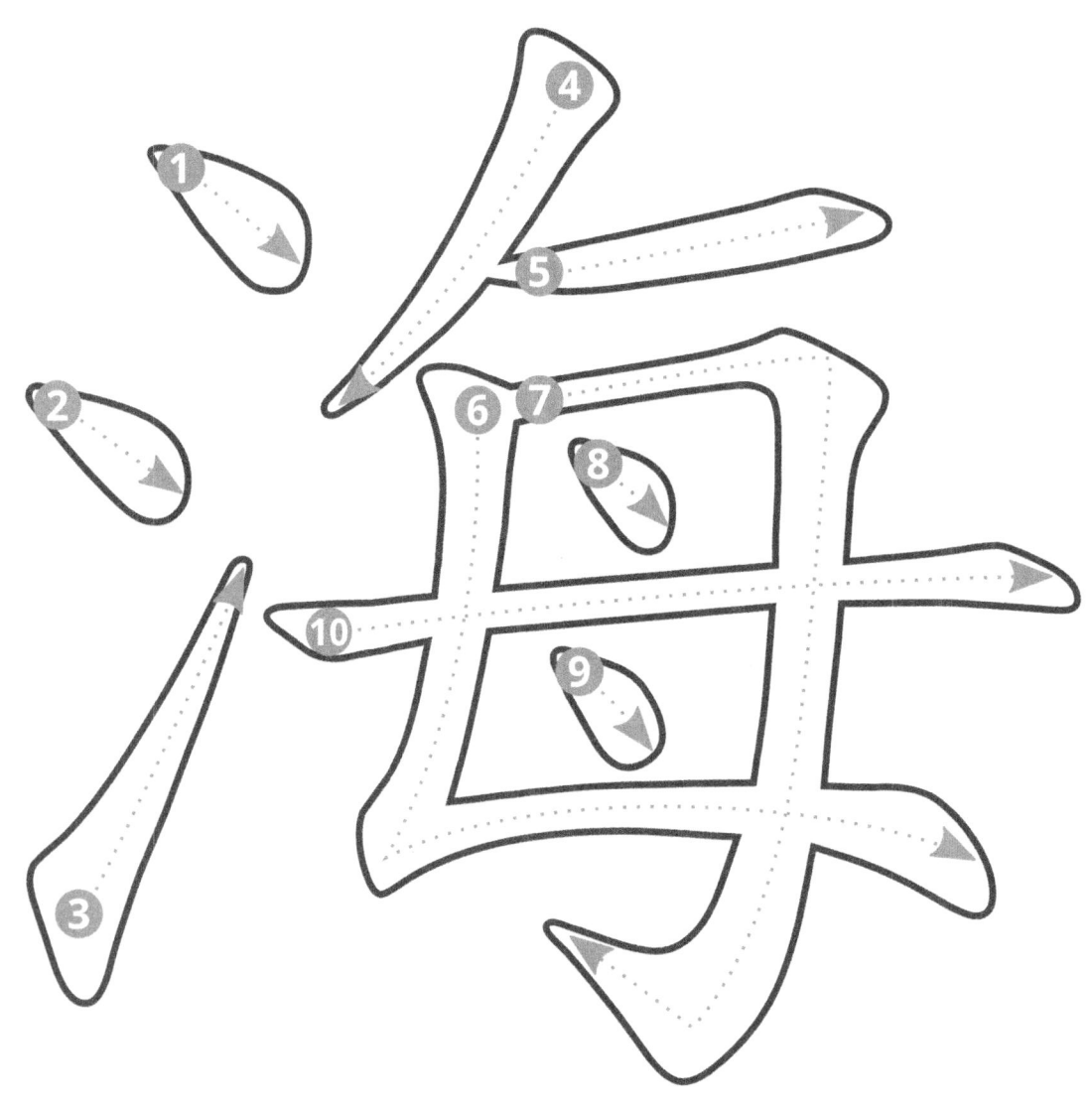

本書中的國字筆順是依據中華民國教育部「常用國字標準字體筆順學習網」的筆劃順序彙編。
The stroke orders of the characters in this workbook follow the stroke orders provided on the "Learning Program for Stroke Order of Frequently Used Chinese Characters" website of the Ministry of Education, R.O.C. (Taiwan).

連連看
Draw lines to the matching objects.

山 •   •

海 •   •

雲 •   •

樹 •   •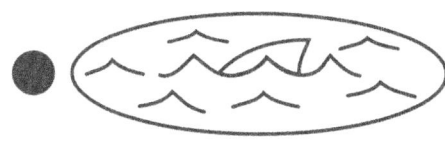

唸出下面的文字並完成圖案。
Read aloud the characters below and complete the picture.

海裡有很多魚

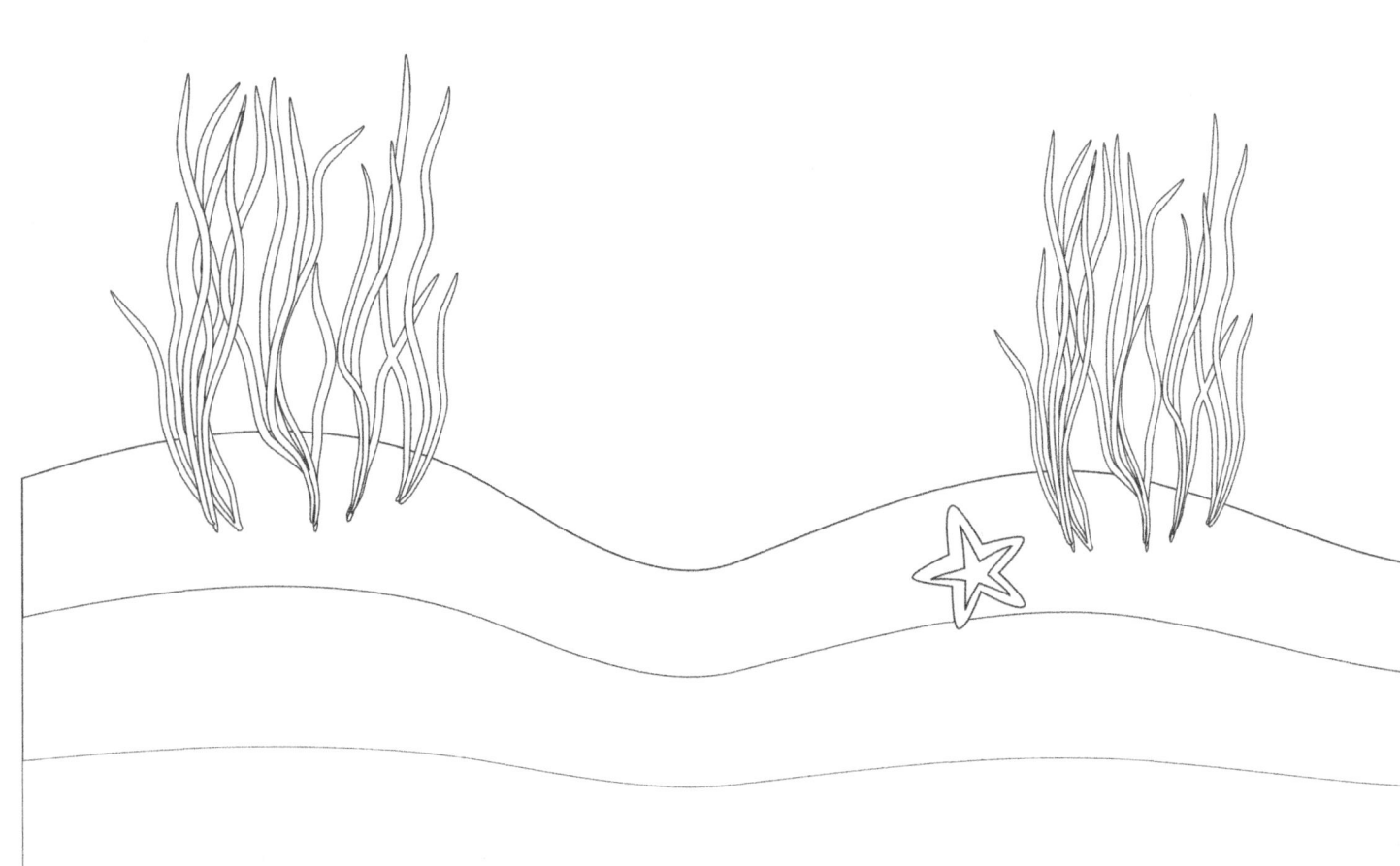

唸唸看
Read-Aloud

- 老師讓我們回家想一想對於這次的校外教學有什麼看法。
The teacher lets us go home to think about what we think about the field trip this time.

- 我很喜歡這次的教學，因為要去海邊。
I like this field trip because (we) are going to the beach.

- 小明不太滿意，因為他怕海裡有怪物會把他當食物吃了。
Ming is not very happy because he is afraid there will be a monster in the ocean that will eat him.

- 老師說：「哪會有怪物這種東西？你聽誰說的？」
The teacher says, "There is no such thing as a monster. Who did you hear it from?"

- 小明說：「我最近看太多電視了。」
Ming says, "I watched too much television recently."

恭喜你完成了這一課，請回到第一頁將本課的吊鐘塗上顏色。
Congratulations! You have completed a lesson. Please color the bell for this lesson on page 1.

第三課

Lesson 3 Biàn – informal; convenient; to urinate or defecate; in that case
Pián – cheap; inexpensive

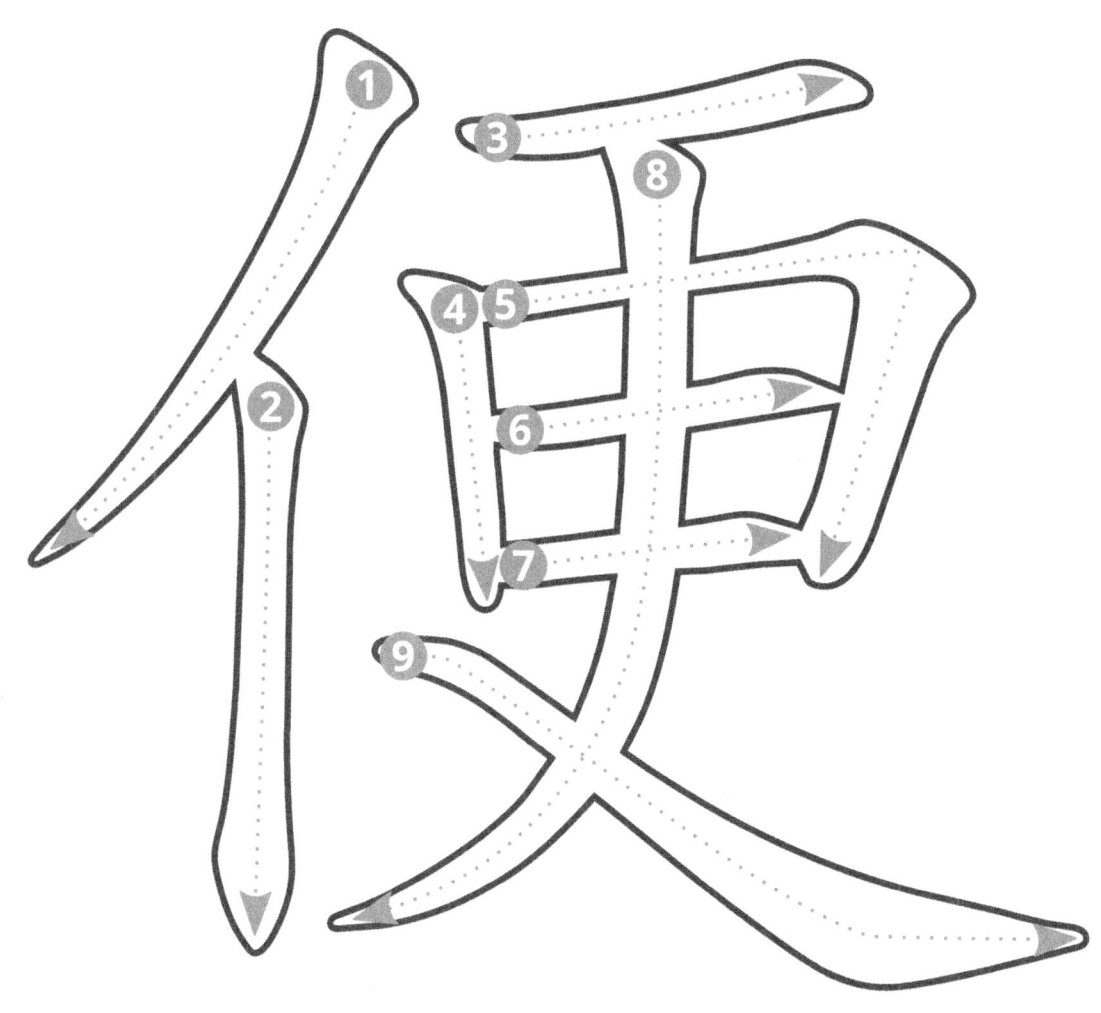

本書中的國字筆順是依據中華民國教育部「常用國字標準字體筆順學習網」的筆劃順序彙編。
The stroke orders of the characters in this workbook follow the stroke orders provided on the "Learning Program for Stroke Order of Frequently Used Chinese Characters" website of the Ministry of Education, R.O.C. (Taiwan).

請把有「便」字的地方著色。
Please color the ares with the character 便.

12

請將下方的字格剪下來讓孩子選擇正確的字貼上。
Please cut out the characters at the bottom and paste the correct one.

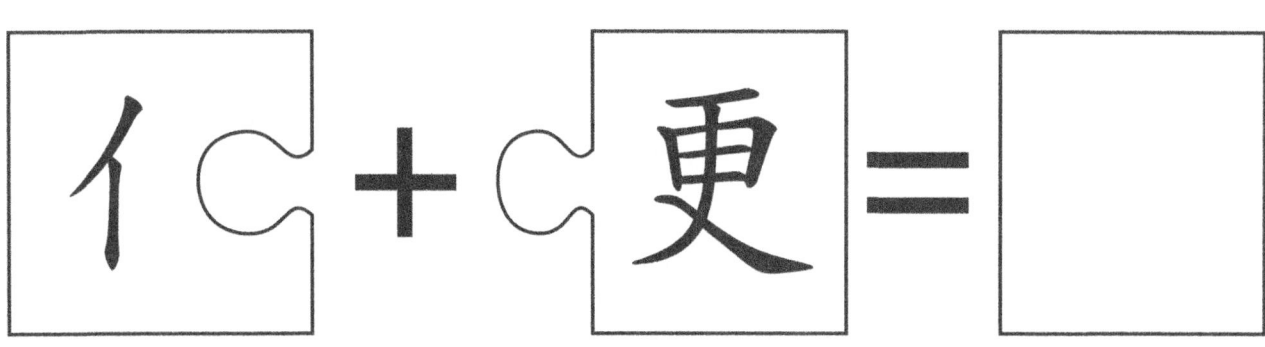

| 亻 | 梗 | 更 | 便 | 硬 |

唸唸看
Read-Aloud

- 今天老師帶著我們離開都市去海邊。
Today the teacher took us away from the city to the beach.

- 由於是校外教學老師讓我們穿便服。
Because it is a field trip, the teacher lets us dress in casual outfits.

- 海邊離學校很遠，來回非常不方便。
The beach is far away from the school. It is not convenient to go to.

- 開車一來一往要三小時左右。
A trip driving back and forth will be about three hours.

- 就算很遠我還是很快樂，因為我最喜歡大海了。
Even though (it) is very far, I am still very happy because the ocean is my favorite.

恭喜你完成了這一課，請回到第一頁將本課的吊鐘塗上顏色。
Congratulations! You have completed a lesson. Please color the bell for this lesson on page 1.

第四課

Lesson 4 Rè – to warm up; to heat up; hot (of weather); heat; fervent

本書中的國字筆順是依據中華民國教育部「常用國字標準字體筆順學習網」的筆劃順序彙編。
The stroke orders of the characters in this workbook follow the stroke orders provided on the "Learning Program for Stroke Order of Frequently Used Chinese Characters" website of the Ministry of Education, R.O.C. (Taiwan).

在熱的物品旁貼上「熱」字。
Paste the character 熱 next to things that are hot.

16

圖案中有的東西在（ ）中打勾。
Put a check next to the items that are in the picture.

（ ）天空 （ ）小鳥 （ ）水
（ ）山   （ ）雲   （ ）熱氣球

唸唸看
Read-Aloud

- 天氣熱的時候我喜歡去海邊玩水。
When the weather is hot, I like to go to the beach to play with water.

- 有一次我在海邊玩，小鳥的大便落到了我的頭上。
One time (when) I was playing at the beach, a little bird's poop dropped on my head.

- 有一個熱心的老奶奶幫我清理頭上的鳥大便。
A zealous old granny helped me clean up the bird poop on my head.

- 老奶奶還給了我一杯水喝和一些點心吃。
The old granny also gave me a cup of water to drink and some dessert to eat.

- 老奶奶人真好。
The old granny is very nice.

恭喜你完成了這一課，請回到第一頁將本課的吊鐘塗上顏色。
Congratulations! You have completed a lesson. Please color the bell for this lesson on page 1.

第五課

Lesson 5 Bèi – quilt; by; (indicates passive-voice clauses)

本書中的國字筆順是依據中華民國教育部「常用國字標準字體筆順學習網」的筆劃順序彙編。
The stroke orders of the characters in this workbook follow the stroke orders provided on the "Learning Program for Stroke Order of Frequently Used Chinese Characters" website of the Ministry of Education, R.O.C. (Taiwan).

請將三個相同的字連成一線。
Please connect the same characters to win the tic-tac-toe.

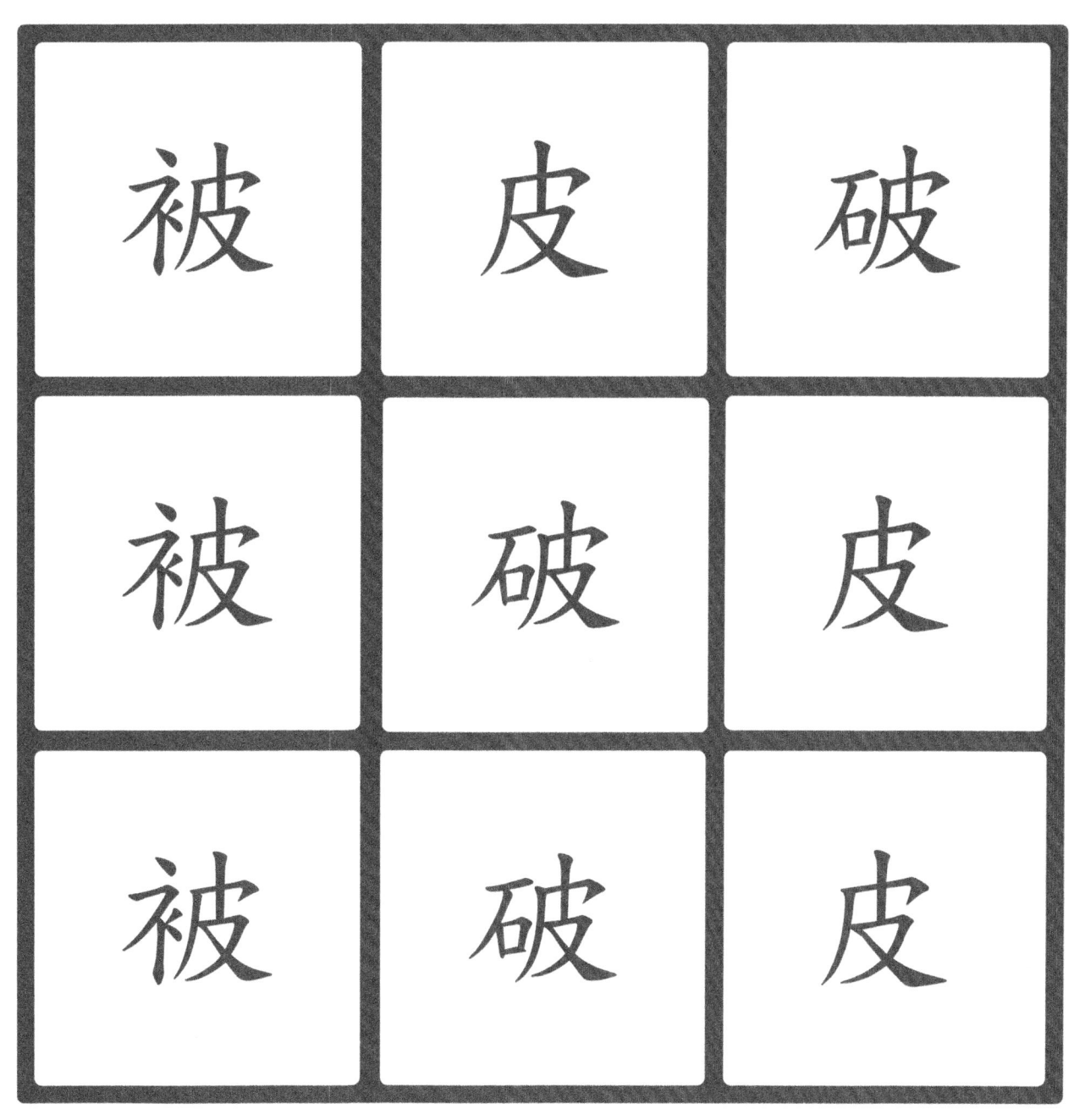

20

將「被」字塗色，幫烏龜找到朋友。
Color the characters 被 to help the tortoise find its friend.

		皮		
被	被	被		
			之	
彼		被	被	被
熱		坡		被
海		便	歡	破	被
喜				被

唸唸看
Read-Aloud

- 前天晚上睡覺時我做了一個夢。
When I was sleeping the night before yesterday, I had a dream.

- 夢裡我被熱氣球帶上藍藍的天空中。
In the dream I was taken up to the blue sky by a hot air balloon.

- 熱氣球帶著我飛過高山、穿越白雲，來到一片綠色的草地。
The hot air balloon took me across high mountains, through white clouds, and arrived at a green field.

- 正要安全落地時我便被爸爸叫起來了。
Just when I was safely landing, I was woken by Dad.

- 我好喜歡這個夢，我把它寫在日記裡。
I liked this dream very much. I wrote it in the diary.

恭喜你完成了這一課，請回到第一頁將本課的吊鐘塗上顏色。
Congratulations! You have completed a lesson. Please color the bell for this lesson on page 1.

第六課

Lesson 6 Bié – to leave; to depart; to separate; to distinguish; to classify; other; another; don't …!; to pin

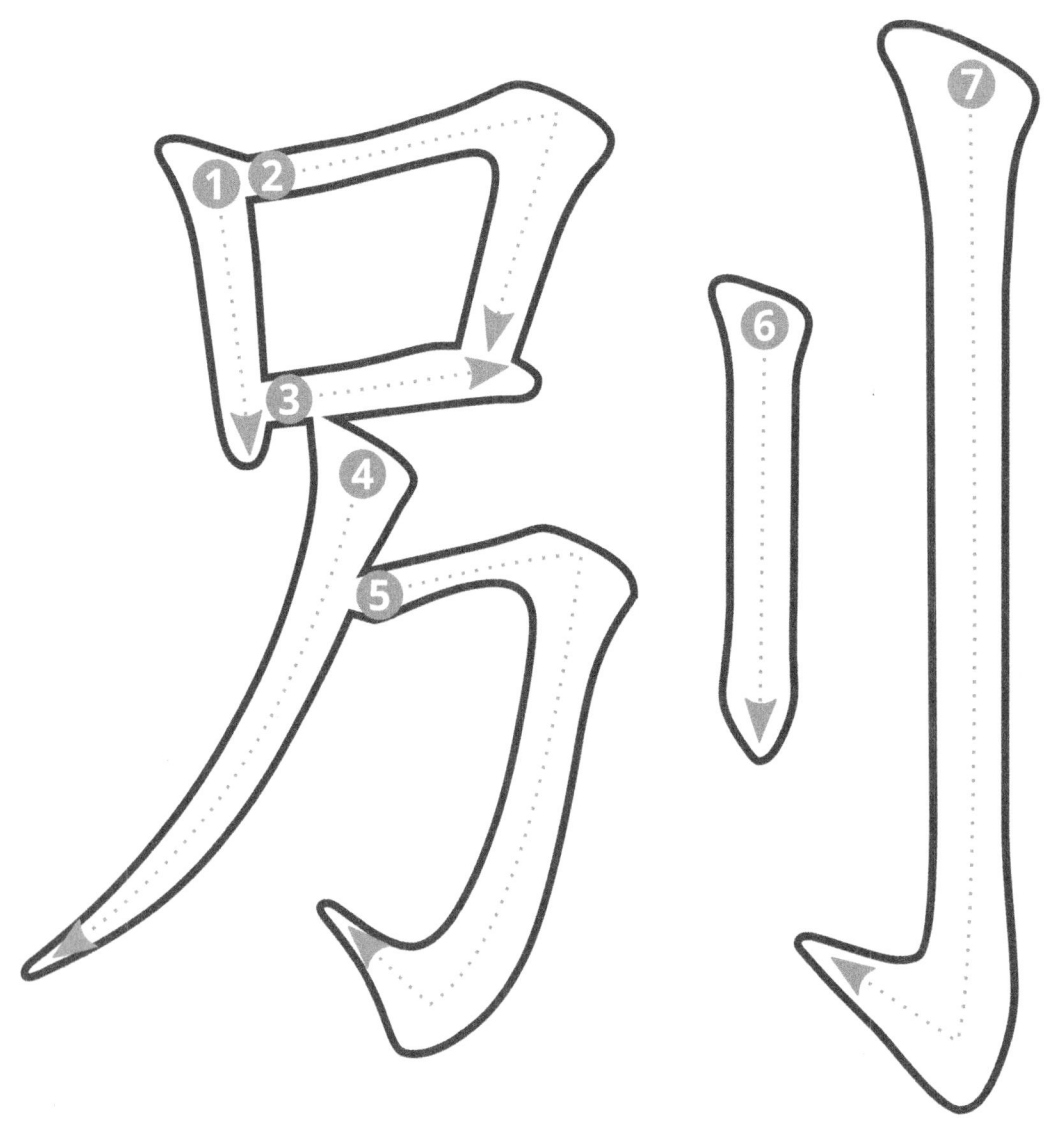

本書中的國字筆順是依據中華民國教育部「常用國字標準字體筆順學習網」的筆劃順序彙編。
The stroke orders of the characters in this workbook follow the stroke orders provided on the "Learning Program for Stroke Order of Frequently Used Chinese Characters" website of the Ministry of Education, R.O.C. (Taiwan).

找出「別」字圈出來。
Find the characters 別 and circle them.

別　　　　　被

　另　　　別

　力

　　便　　別

　熱　　　歡

跟著「別」字從 ➡ 到 ★ 走出迷宮。
Follow the characters 別 from the arrow to the star to exit the maze.

別	力	也	安	左
別	喜	的	到	右
別	別	別	口	相
另	被	別	便	熱
海	歡	別	別	別

唸唸看
Read-Aloud

- 弟弟問表姐為什麼有海牛和海馬，但是沒有海豬呢？

  (My) younger brother asked (my) elder female cousin why there are manatees and seahorses but no sea pigs?

- 弟弟又問為什麼有熱狗，可是沒有熱貓呢？

  (My) younger brother asked again why there are hot dogs but no hot cats?

- 他還問為什麼有大便和小便，而沒有中便呢？

  He also asked why there are poop (big ones) and pee (small ones), but no middle ones.

- 表姐笑著說別問她，因為她也不知道。

  (My) elder female cousin smiled and said don't ask her because she doesn't know either.

- 弟弟只好改問別人了。

  (My) younger brother has to ask someone else.

恭喜你完成了這一課，請回到第一頁將本課的吊鐘塗上顏色。
Congratulations! You have completed a lesson. Please color the bell for this lesson on page 1.

第七課

Lesson 7 Zhuā – to grab; to catch; to arrest; to snatch; to scratch

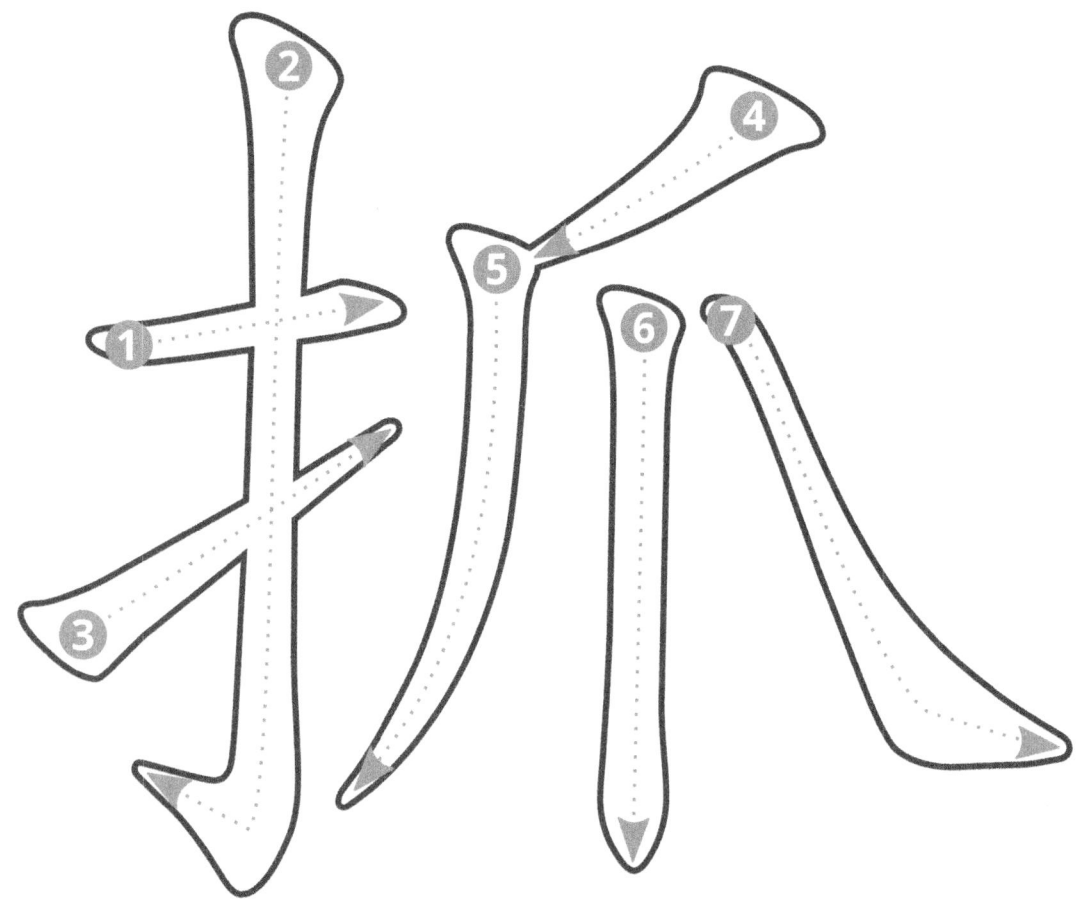

本書中的國字筆順是依據中華民國教育部「常用國字標準字體筆順學習網」的筆劃順序彙編。
The stroke orders of the characters in this workbook follow the stroke orders provided on the "Learning Program for Stroke Order of Frequently Used Chinese Characters" website of the Ministry of Education, R.O.C. (Taiwan).

請在與圖案相對應的句子前面打勾。
Put a checkmark in front of the phrase that best describes the picture.

（　）天亮了，太陽出來了。

（　）小貓想要抓小鳥。

（　）我的頭很大。

（　）我找不到他。

閱讀測驗。請在正確答案的前面打勾。
Read the following paragraph and answer the questions below.

公主又被壞人抓走了。王子這次不想去打壞人。小明說他去。結果小明也被壞人抓了起來。最後王子還是得出馬。

1. 小明為什麼會被抓起來？
　（　）公主不喜歡小明
　（　）小明打不過壞人
　（　）王子叫壞人把小明抓起來

2. 這裡出馬的意思是？
　（　）去打壞人
　（　）馬上出發
　（　）去打小明

3. 說出你覺得故事最後怎樣了？

唸唸看
Read-Aloud

- 今天天氣太熱了，實在受不了。
  Today the weather is too hot. I can't stand it.

- 我們一起去河邊抓魚吧。
  Let's go to the riverside to catch fish.

- 我們花了好長的時間才到目的地。
  We spent a long time reaching the destination.

- 到了以後我們才發現全部的魚都被別人抓光了。
  After arriving we realized that other people caught all the fish, and there were none left.

- 最終我們一條都沒抓到便回家了。
  In the end we didn't catch even one fish and went home.

恭喜你完成了這一課，請回到第一頁將本課的吊鐘塗上顏色。
Congratulations! You have completed a lesson. Please color the bell for this lesson on page 1.

第八課
Lesson 8 Jué – to decide; to determine; definitely; certainly

本書中的國字筆順是依據中華民國教育部「常用國字標準字體筆順學習網」的筆劃順序彙編。
The stroke orders of the characters in this workbook follow the stroke orders provided on the "Learning Program for Stroke Order of Frequently Used Chinese Characters" website of the Ministry of Education, R.O.C. (Taiwan).

請將有「決」字的企鵝著色。
Please color the penguins with the character 決.

32

請將下方的字格剪下來選擇正確的字貼上。
Please cut out the characters at the bottom and paste the correct ones.

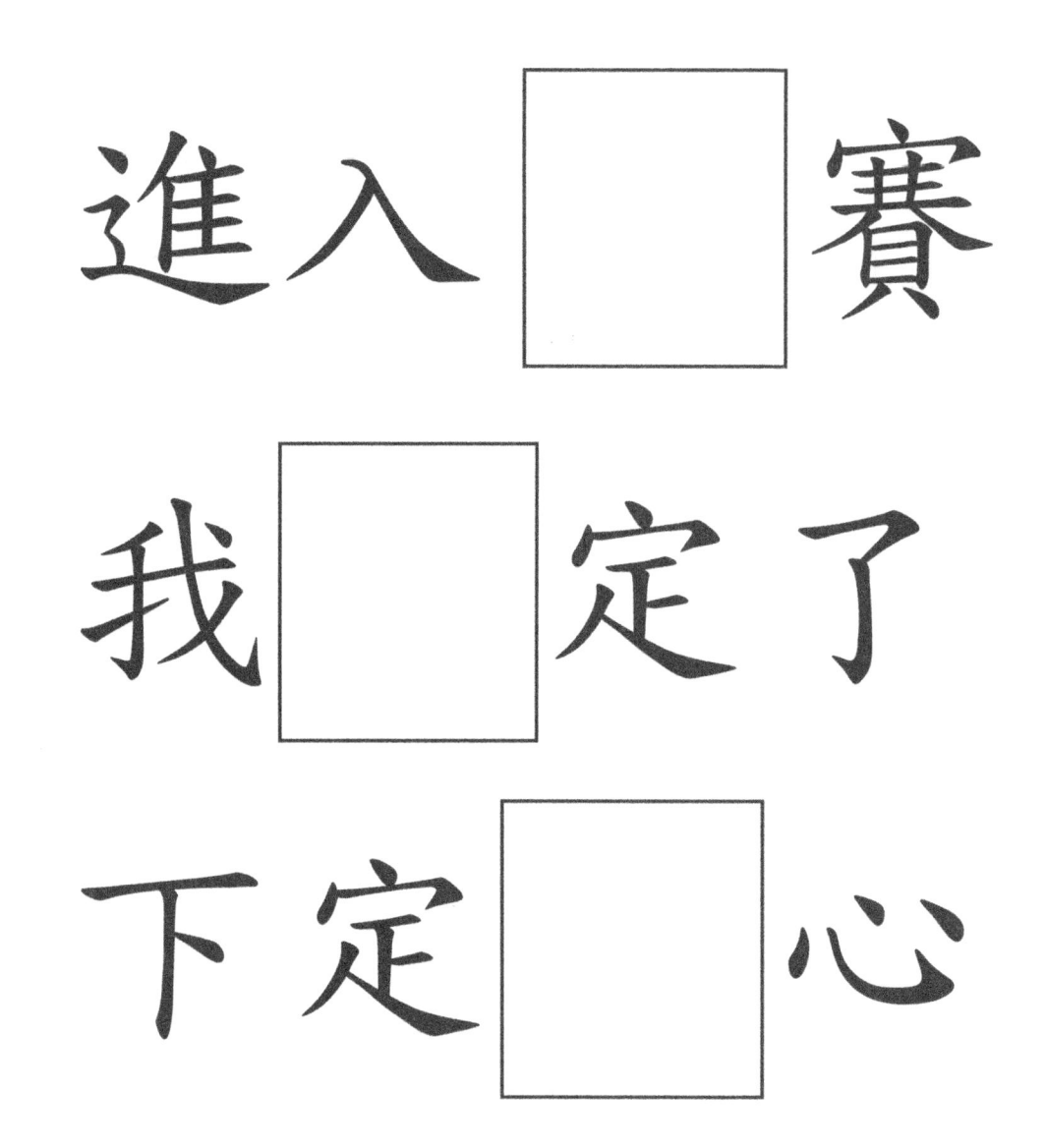

進入 ☐ 賽

我 ☐ 定了

下定 ☐ 心

決　快　決　決　決

唸唸看
Read-Aloud

- 太陽很大天氣又熱了，我們決定去看電影。

   It is very sunny, and the weather is hot. We decided to go to the movies.

- 公主坐在花園的樹下被壞人抓走了，而且哭得很傷心。

   The princess was sitting under the tree in the garden (when she) was taken away by the bad guys, and (she) cried sadly.

- 王子下定決心要打倒壞人。

   The prince decided to defeat the bad guy.

- 妹妹看電影時不停地說話。

   (My) younger sister didn't stop talking when (she) was seeing the movie.

- 我跟她說在電影院看電影別說話。

   I told her not to talk when seeing a movie at the movie theater.

恭喜你完成了這一課，請回到第一頁將本課的吊鐘塗上顏色。
Congratulations! You have completed a lesson. Please color the bell for this lesson on page 1.

第九課

Lesson 9 Zǒng – always; total; overall; head; chief; general

本書中的國字筆順是依據中華民國教育部「常用國字標準字體筆順學習網」的筆劃順序彙編。
The stroke orders of the characters in this workbook follow the stroke orders provided on the "Learning Program for Stroke Order of Frequently Used Chinese Characters" website of the Ministry of Education, R.O.C. (Taiwan).

閱讀測驗。請在正確答案的前面打勾。
Read the following paragraph and answer the questions below.

我總是回家後先把功課寫完才出去玩。小明總是等到睡覺前才一邊哭一邊寫功課。

1. 誰回家會先寫功課？
   （ ）我　（ ）妹妹　（ ）小明
2. 小明為什麼一邊哭一邊寫功課？
   （ ）功課太難寫
   （ ）要睡覺了寫功課的時間不夠
   （ ）小明本來就很愛哭
3. 你覺得誰是好學生？
   （ ）小明
   （ ）我
   （ ）大明

36

唸出下面的文字並完成任務。
Read aloud the characters below and complete the task.

數一數總共有幾隻貓？

唸唸看
Read-Aloud

- 我一早帶著弟弟坐公車去看足球總決賽。
Early in the morning, I took (my) younger brother to ride the bus to watch the final soccer game.

- 弟弟向來愛跑在前面，也不等等我。
(My) younger brother always likes to run in the front and not wait for me.

- 今天他上錯公車被我拉了下來。
Today he went on the wrong bus and was dragged down by me.

- 我抓著他的手說小心別上錯車了。
I grabbed his hand and said be careful not to get on the wrong bus.

- 要是錯過總決賽心情一定會不好。
If (we) missed the finals, (we) will definitely be in a bad mood.

恭喜你完成了這一課，請回到第一頁將本課的吊鐘塗上顏色。
Congratulations! You have completed a lesson. Please color the bell for this lesson on page 1.

第十課

Lesson 10 Mǐ – rice; meter (classifier)

本書中的國字筆順是依據中華民國教育部「常用國字標準字體筆順學習網」的筆劃順序彙編。
The stroke orders of the characters in this workbook follow the stroke orders provided on the "Learning Program for Stroke Order of Frequently Used Chinese Characters" website of the Ministry of Education, R.O.C. (Taiwan).

請把「米」字連到用米做的食物。
Please connect the character to the foods that are made of rice.

米

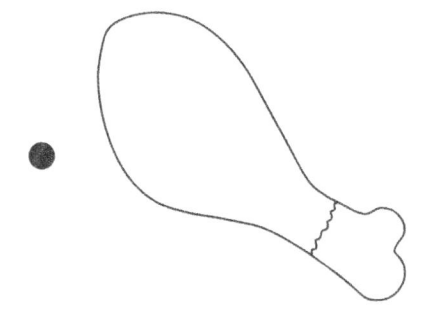

40

請將有「米」字的米袋著色。
Please color the bags with the character 米.

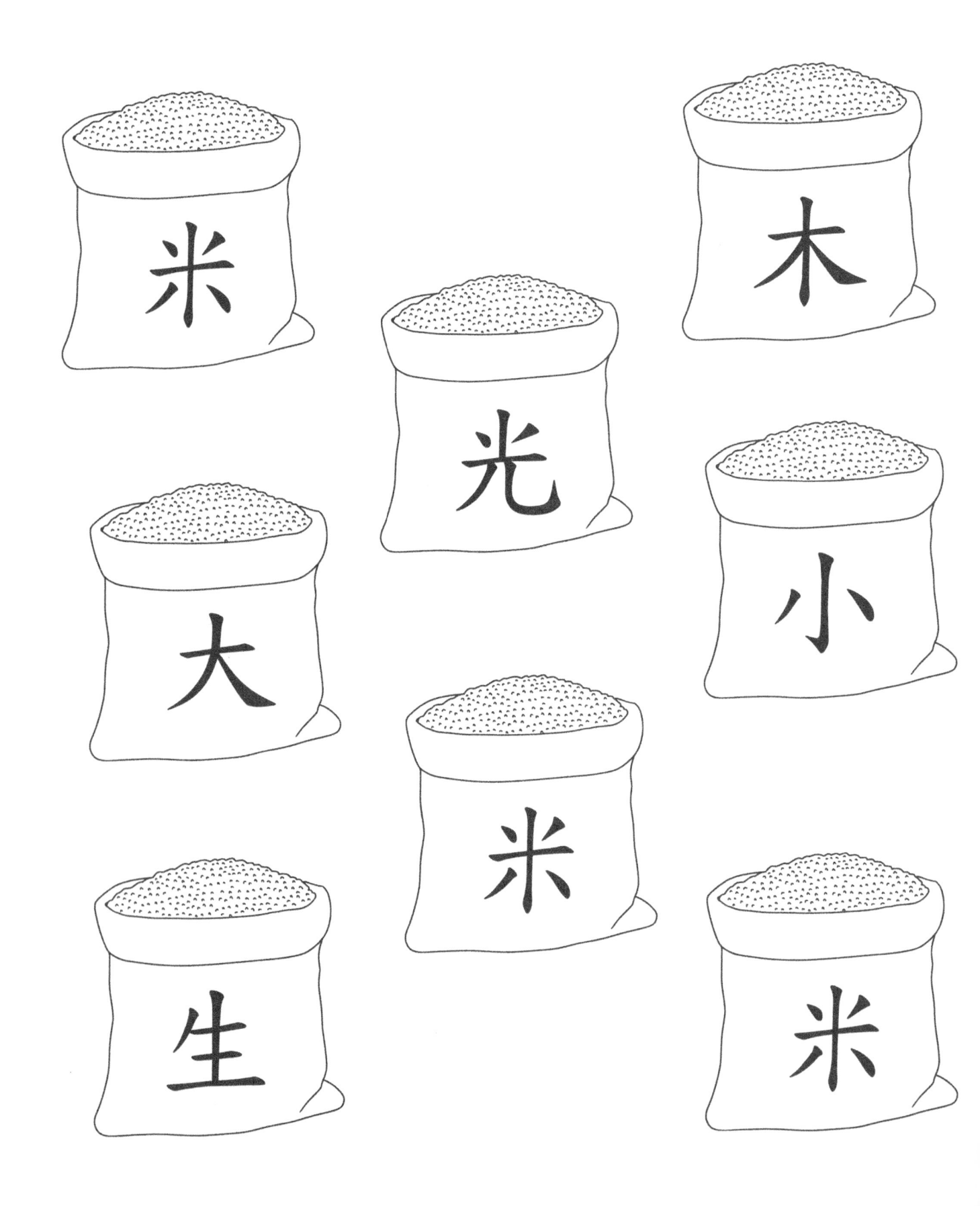

唸唸看
Read-Aloud

- 在球場看總決賽時，弟弟拿出了一把花生米。
  When watching the finals at the sports field, (my) younger brother took out a handful of peanuts.

- 我問：「你怎麼會有花生米？」
  I asked, "Why do you have peanuts?"

- 他說：「我出門前抓了一把，不要跟別人說。」
  He said, "When I left (the house), I grabbed a handful. Don't tell others."

- 我說：「你可以分給我一半嗎？」
  I said, "Can you share half with me?"

- 弟弟說：「當然可以！」
  (My) younger brother said, "Of course!"

恭喜你完成了這一課，請回到第一頁將本課的吊鐘塗上顏色。
Congratulations! You have completed a lesson. Please color the bell for this lesson on page 1.

第十一課

Lesson 11 Bǎi – hundred; numerous; all kinds of

本書中的國字筆順是依據中華民國教育部「常用國字標準字體筆順學習網」的筆劃順序彙編。
The stroke orders of the characters in this workbook follow the stroke orders provided on the "Learning Program for Stroke Order of Frequently Used Chinese Characters" website of the Ministry of Education, R.O.C. (Taiwan).

請圈出正確的數值。
Please circle the correct value.

$500 　　　五百／一百

$100 　　　五百／一百

$100 $100 $100 $100 $100 　　　五百／一百

$100 $100 $500 　　　三百／七百

44

請剪下下方的字格並依照數字由小到大的順序貼到車箱上。
Please cut out the characters at the bottom and paste them in the order from the smallest to the largest number onto the train.

三百　五十　一百

唸唸看
Read-Aloud

- 去年哥哥在百米賽跑總決賽得到第二名。
Last year (my) elder brother got second place at the 100 meters final race.

- 今年總共有好幾百人來看總決賽。
This year there are hundreds of people coming to see the final race.

- 能夠進入總決賽的人應該都跑得很快。
People that can enter the final race should all be able to run fast.

- 我相信哥哥今年有機會得到第一名。
I believe (my) elder brother has a chance to get first place this year.

- 因為他喜歡的女孩有來現場看他比賽。
Because the girl he likes is here to watch him race.

恭喜你完成了這一課，請回到第一頁將本課的吊鐘塗上顏色。
Congratulations! You have completed a lesson. Please color the bell for this lesson on page 1.

第十二課

Lesson 12 Liàn – to practice; to train; to drill

本書中的國字筆順是依據中華民國教育部「常用國字標準字體筆順學習網」的筆劃順序彙編。
The stroke orders of the characters in this workbook follow the stroke orders provided on the "Learning Program for Stroke Order of Frequently Used Chinese Characters" website of the Ministry of Education, R.O.C. (Taiwan).

請將三個相同的字連成一線。
Please connect the same characters to win the tic-tac-toe.

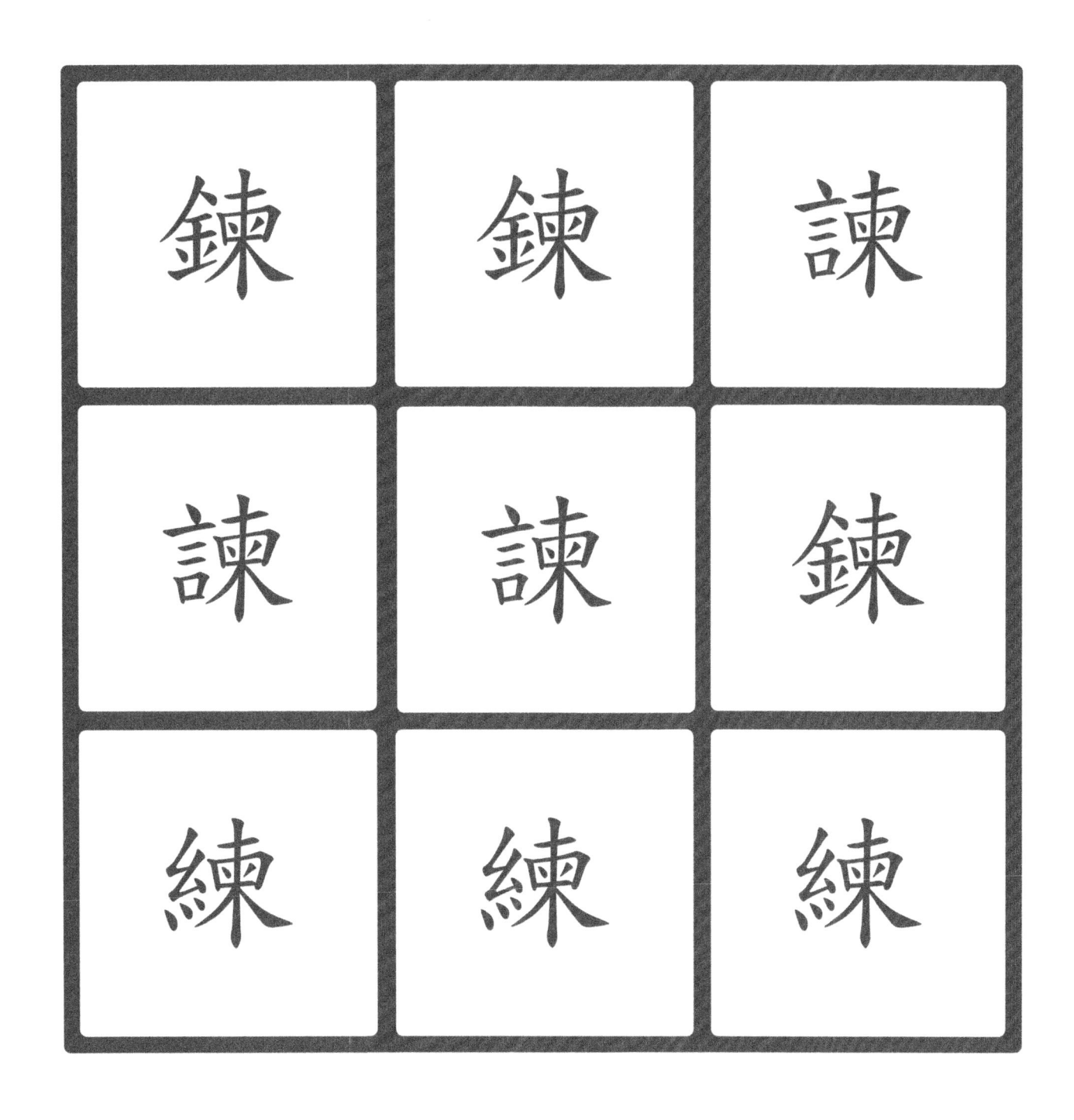

鍊	鍊	諫
諫	諫	鍊
練	練	練

找出「練」字圈出來。
Find the characters 練 and circle them.

別   鞋

諫   練

束   總

練

百   抓

練   鍊

唸唸看
Read-Aloud

- 自從哥哥百米賽跑總決賽得到第一名以後，他就越來越熱愛運動。
Ever since (my) elder brother got first place in the 100 meters final race, he loves to exercise more and more.

- 拿到第一名讓他很有成就感。
Getting first place makes him feel accomplished.

- 哥哥每天會先練跑步，再和隊友一塊兒練球。
Everyday (my) elder brother will first practice running and then practice ball with (his) teammates.

- 妹妹的聲音很好聽，她每天都要練唱好幾首歌。
(My) younger sister's voice is very pleasant, she practices singing many songs everyday.

- 我每天都自己練書法，要寫好多個字。
I practice writing calligraphy by myself everyday. (I) need to write many characters.

恭喜你完成了這一課，請回到第一頁將本課的吊鐘塗上顏色。
Congratulations! You have completed a lesson. Please color the bell for this lesson on page 1.

第十三課

Lesson 13 Xí – to practice; to study; habit

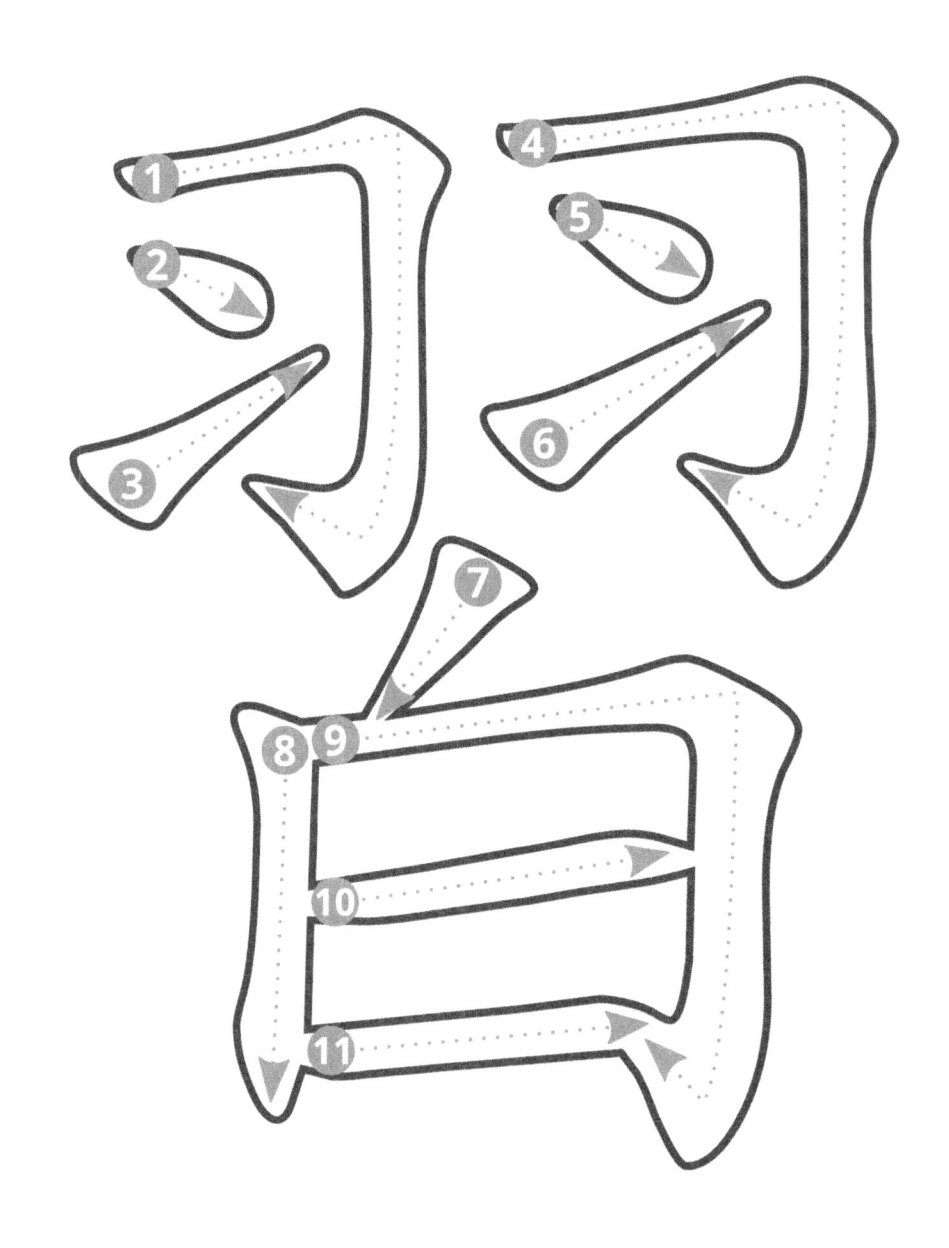

本書中的國字筆順是依據中華民國教育部「常用國字標準字體筆順學習網」的筆劃順序彙編。
The stroke orders of the characters in this workbook follow the stroke orders provided on the "Learning Program for Stroke Order of Frequently Used Chinese Characters" website of the Ministry of Education, R.O.C. (Taiwan).

閱讀測驗。請在正確答案的前面打勾。
Read the following paragraph and answer the questions below.

小美的字寫得很好看,因為她每天都練習寫書法。小麗的歌唱得很好,因為她每天都要練唱。

1. 小麗很會唱歌是因為?
   (　) 每天寫書法
   (　) 每天出去玩
   (　) 每天練唱

2. 本文想要讓你知道什麼?
   (　) 學任何東西只要經常練習就會越來越進步。
   (　) 字要寫得好看一定要先學會書法。

52

跟著「習」字從 ➡ 到 ★ 走出迷宮。
Follow the characters 習 from the arrow to the star to exit the maze.

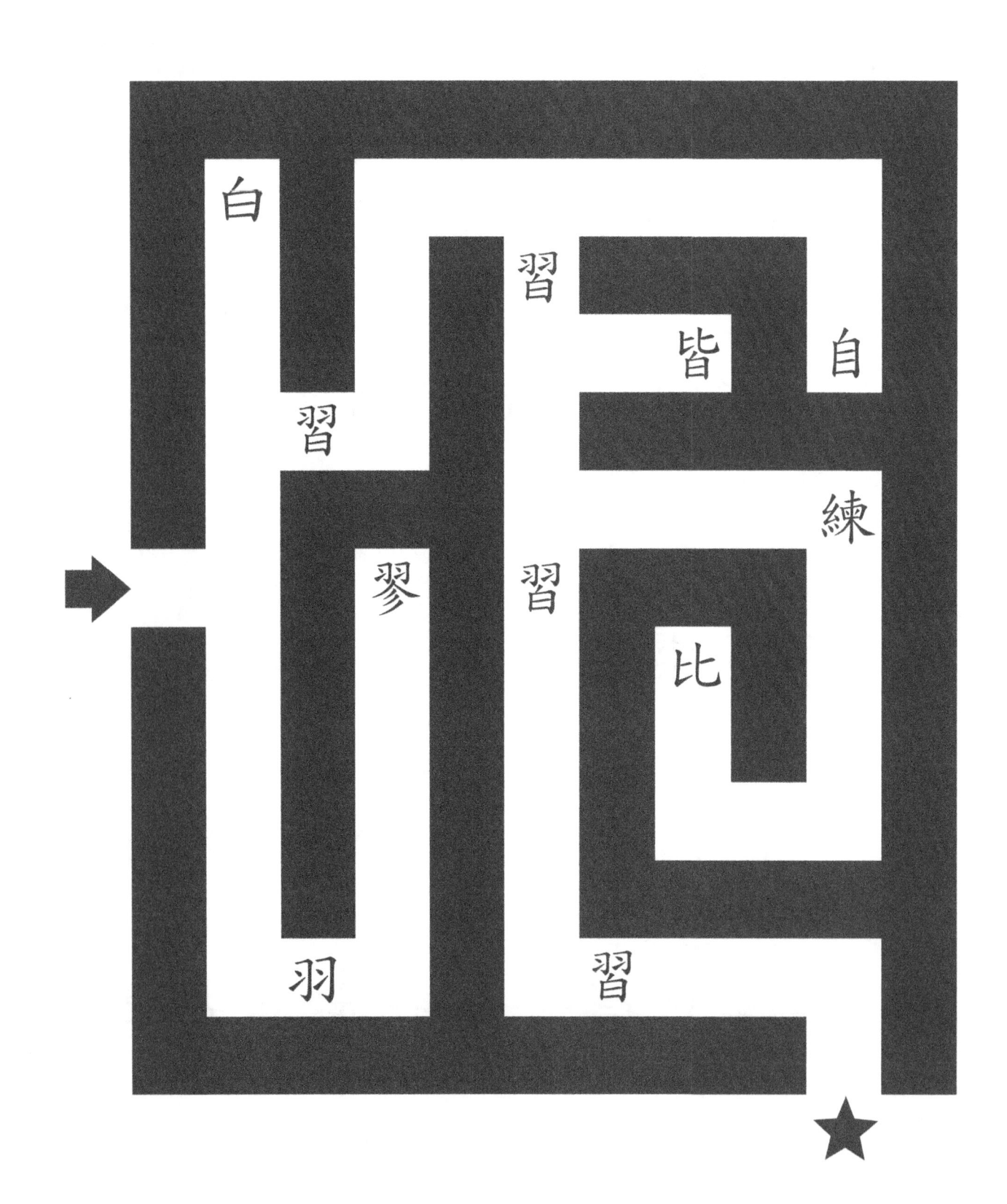

唸唸看
Read-Aloud

- 哥哥總是在放學之後練習跑步。
  (My) elder brother always practices running after school.

- 他每天都要跑好幾百米的路。
  He has to run hundreds of meters everyday.

- 哥哥的學習也很好，任何題目都難不倒他。
  (My) elder brother is good at his studies too, no problems can challenge him.

- 其實我的功課也很好，常常教同學寫作業。
  Actually, I am good at my studies too. (I) often teach (my) classmates how to do (their) homework.

- 在家還常常幫忙媽媽收衣服。
  (I) also often help Mom put away clothes at home.

恭喜你完成了這一課，請回到第一頁將本課的吊鐘塗上顏色。
Congratulations! You have completed a lesson. Please color the bell for this lesson on page 1.

第十四課

Lesson 14 Xié – shoe

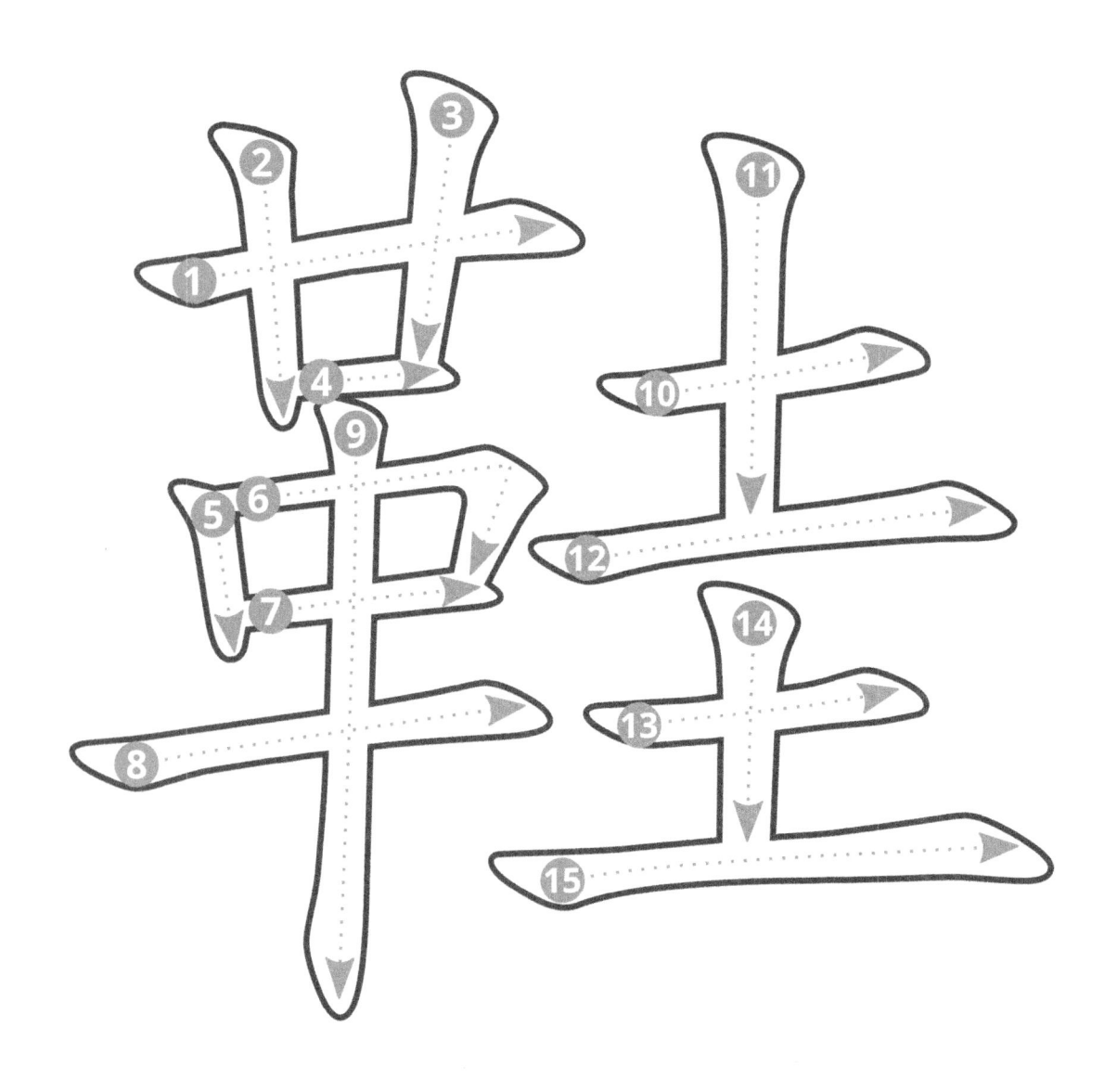

本書中的國字筆順是依據中華民國教育部「常用國字標準字體筆順學習網」的筆劃順序彙編。
The stroke orders of the characters in this workbook follow the stroke orders provided on the "Learning Program for Stroke Order of Frequently Used Chinese Characters" website of the Ministry of Education, R.O.C. (Taiwan).

閱讀測驗。請在正確答案的前面打勾。
Read the following paragraph and answer the questions below.

我家對面開了一家新的鞋店。鞋店裡什麼樣的鞋都有，有大人的、小孩的、男生的、女生的，就是沒有給小狗穿的鞋。

1. 在鞋店買不到什麼鞋？
   ( ) 女生的鞋
   ( ) 小男生的鞋
   ( ) 小狗的鞋
2. 鞋店在哪？
   ( ) 學校對面
   ( ) 我家對面
   ( ) 小明家前面

請跟著小汽車走並唸出路牌上的文字。
Read aloud the signs as the car goes through the road.

鞋子

球鞋

鞋帶

雨鞋

唸唸看
Read-Aloud

- 小美買了新的運動鞋。
  Mei bought new exercise shoes.

- 聽說新鞋賣兩百五十塊。
  (I) heard that the new shoes sell for two hundred and fifty dollars.

- 她穿新鞋練習跑步和跳遠。
  She wore the new shoes to practice running and jumping.

- 不但跳得比較遠,百米比賽的名次也提前了。
  Not only did (she) jumped farther, but (she) even improved her place in the hundred meters race.

- 穿上了五百塊錢的鞋子會不會跑得更快呢?
  Will wearing five-hundred-dollar shoes make (me) run even faster?

恭喜你完成了這一課,請回到第一頁將本課的吊鐘塗上顏色。
Congratulations! You have completed a lesson. Please color the bell for this lesson on page 1.

第十五課

Lesson 15 Shuāng – two; double; pair; both; even (number)

本書中的國字筆順是依據中華民國教育部「常用國字標準字體筆順學習網」的筆劃順序彙編。
The stroke orders of the characters in this workbook follow the stroke orders provided on the "Learning Program for Stroke Order of Frequently Used Chinese Characters" website of the Ministry of Education, R.O.C. (Taiwan).

閱讀測驗。請在正確答案的前面打勾。
Read the following paragraph and answer the questions below.

今天我們全家去買鞋。媽媽買了兩雙鞋。而我買了一雙球鞋。爸爸因為沒有看到喜歡的鞋子，所以沒有買。

1. 誰買最多雙鞋？
   ( ) 媽媽   ( ) 爸爸   ( ) 我
2. 爸爸買了幾雙鞋？
   ( ) 一雙   ( ) 三雙   ( ) 沒有買
3. 爸爸為什麼沒有買？
   ( ) 錢不夠
   ( ) 沒有看到喜歡的
   ( ) 沒法決定買哪雙

60

請按照圖案圈出正確的文字。
Please circle the correct phrases according to the pictures in the boxes.

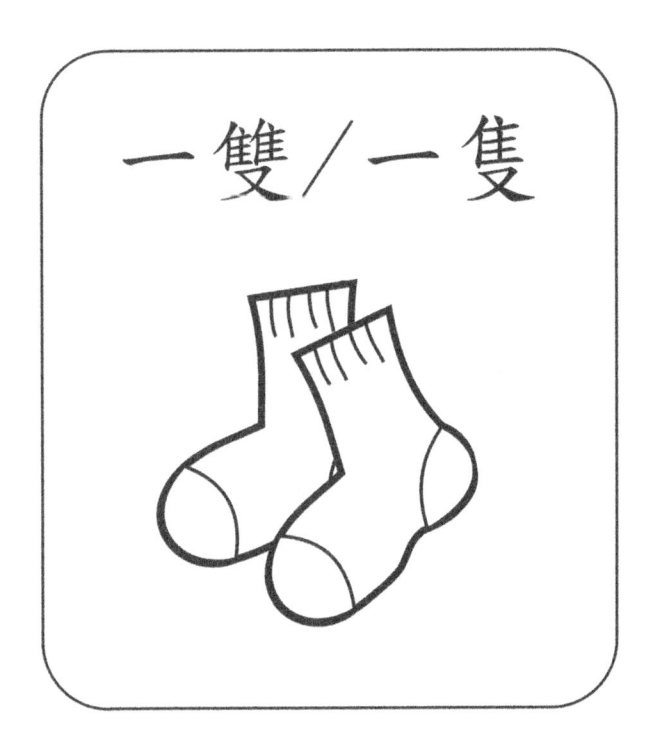

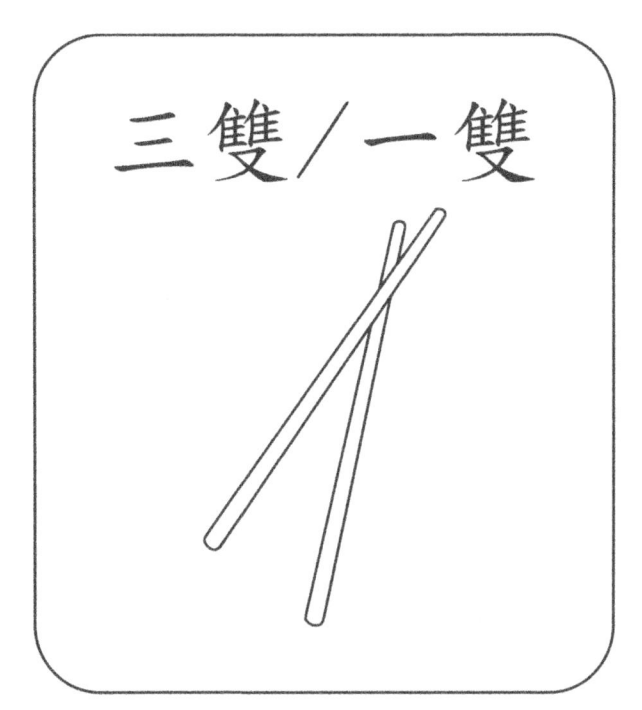

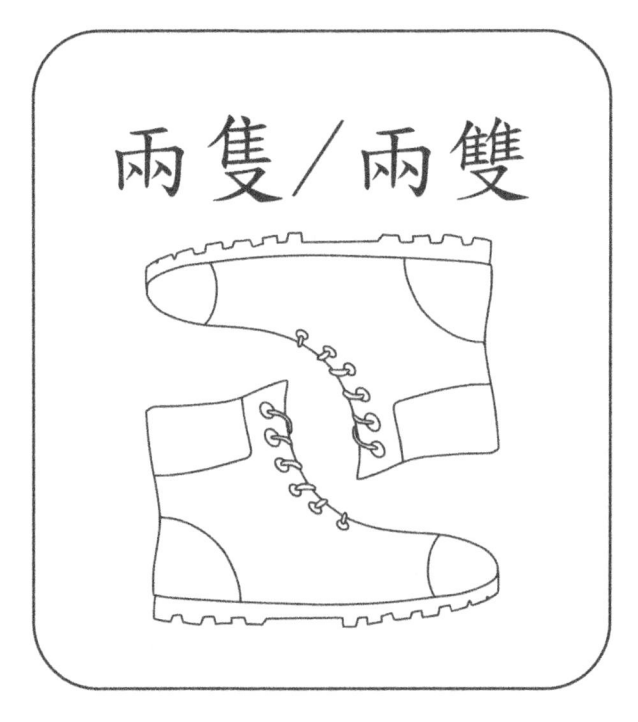

一雙／一隻

三雙／一隻

一雙／一隻

兩隻／兩雙

唸唸看
Read-Aloud

- 鞋店裡有上百雙鞋子。
There are hundreds of pairs of shoes at the shoe store.

- 我喜歡的鞋子有紅色、綠色和灰色。
The shoes I like include red, green, and gray ones.

- 我練習跑步的時候都穿紅色的那雙。
When I practice running, I wear the red pair.

- 我覺得我還少了一雙銀色的鞋子。
I think I am still missing a pair of silver shoes.

- 媽媽說我的鞋子已經多到不行了。
Mom says I have more than enough shoes already.

恭喜你完成了這一課，請回到第一頁將本課的吊鐘塗上顏色。
Congratulations! You have completed a lesson. Please color the bell for this lesson on page 1.

第十六課

Lesson 16 Bù – cloth; to declare; to announce; to spread

本書中的國字筆順是依據中華民國教育部「常用國字標準字體筆順學習網」的筆劃順序彙編。
The stroke orders of the characters in this workbook follow the stroke orders provided on the "Learning Program for Stroke Order of Frequently Used Chinese Characters" website of the Ministry of Education, R.O.C. (Taiwan).

請圈出用布做的東西並唸出下面的文字。
Please circle the items that are made of cloth and read aloud the characters at the bottom.

這些東西都是用布做的

將有「布」字的連身裙著色。
Color the dresses with the character 布.

唸唸看
Read-Aloud

- 姑姑最喜歡那雙白色的布鞋。
  (My) aunt likes that pair of white canvas shoes the best.

- 我也有一雙一樣的白布鞋。
  I also have the same pair of white canvas shoes.

- 我常常穿著它練習跑步。
  I often wear it to practice running.

- 下雨的時候我會穿黃色的雨鞋。
  When (it) rains, I will wear the yellow rain boots.

- 我還有一雙黑色的球鞋，鞋子上面有一顆星星。
  I also have a pair of black sneakers with a star on top.

恭喜你完成了這一課，請回到第一頁將本課的吊鐘塗上顏色。
Congratulations! You have completed a lesson. Please color the bell for this lesson on page 1.

第十七課

Lesson 17 Qí – strange; odd; weird; wonderful; surprisingly; unusually
Jī – odd (number)

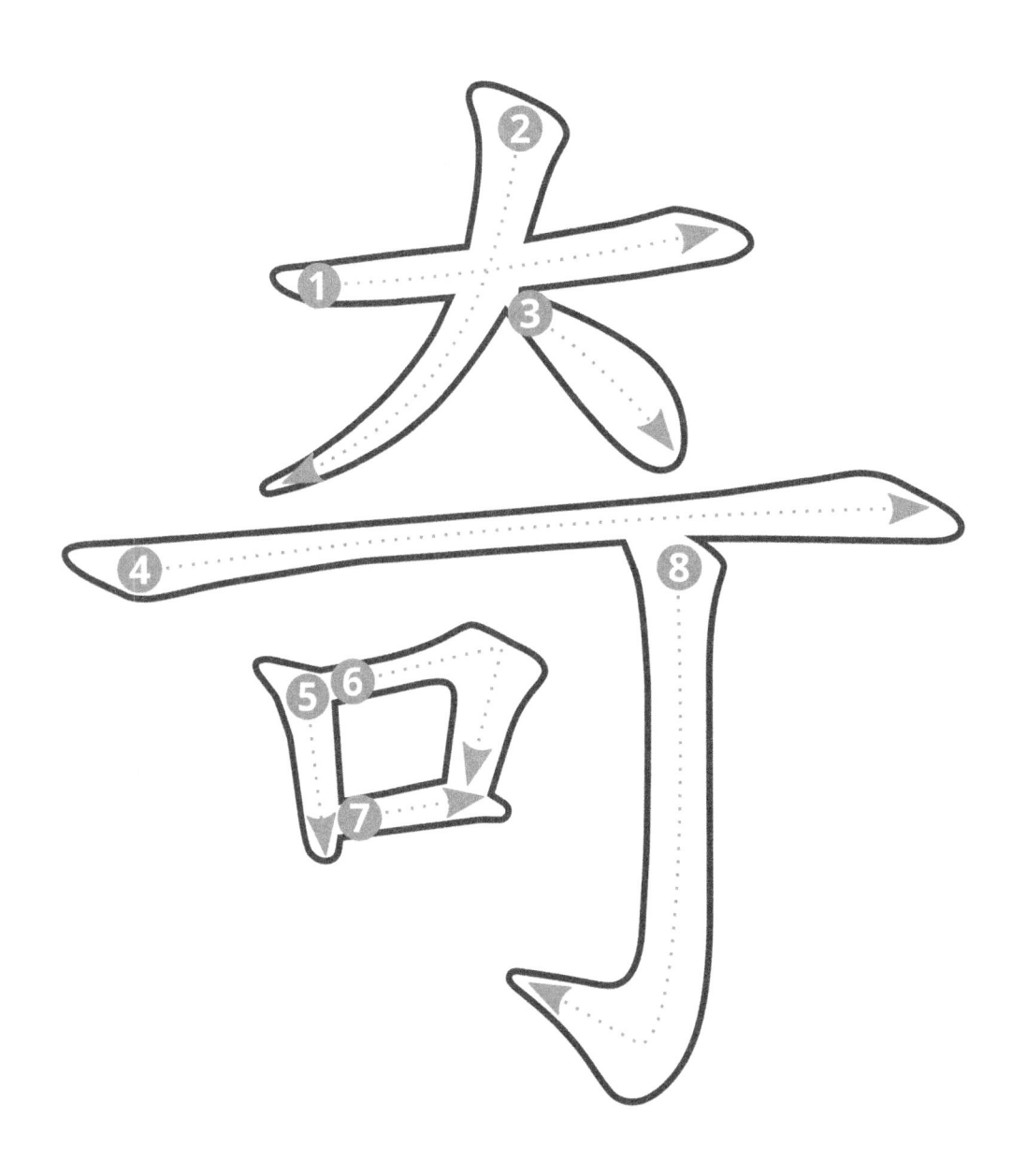

本書中的國字筆順是依據中華民國教育部「常用國字標準字體筆順學習網」的筆劃順序彙編。
The stroke orders of the characters in this workbook follow the stroke orders provided on the "Learning Program for Stroke Order of Frequently Used Chinese Characters" website of the Ministry of Education, R.O.C. (Taiwan).

請將有「奇」字的冰淇淋著色。
Please color the ice cream cones with the character 奇.

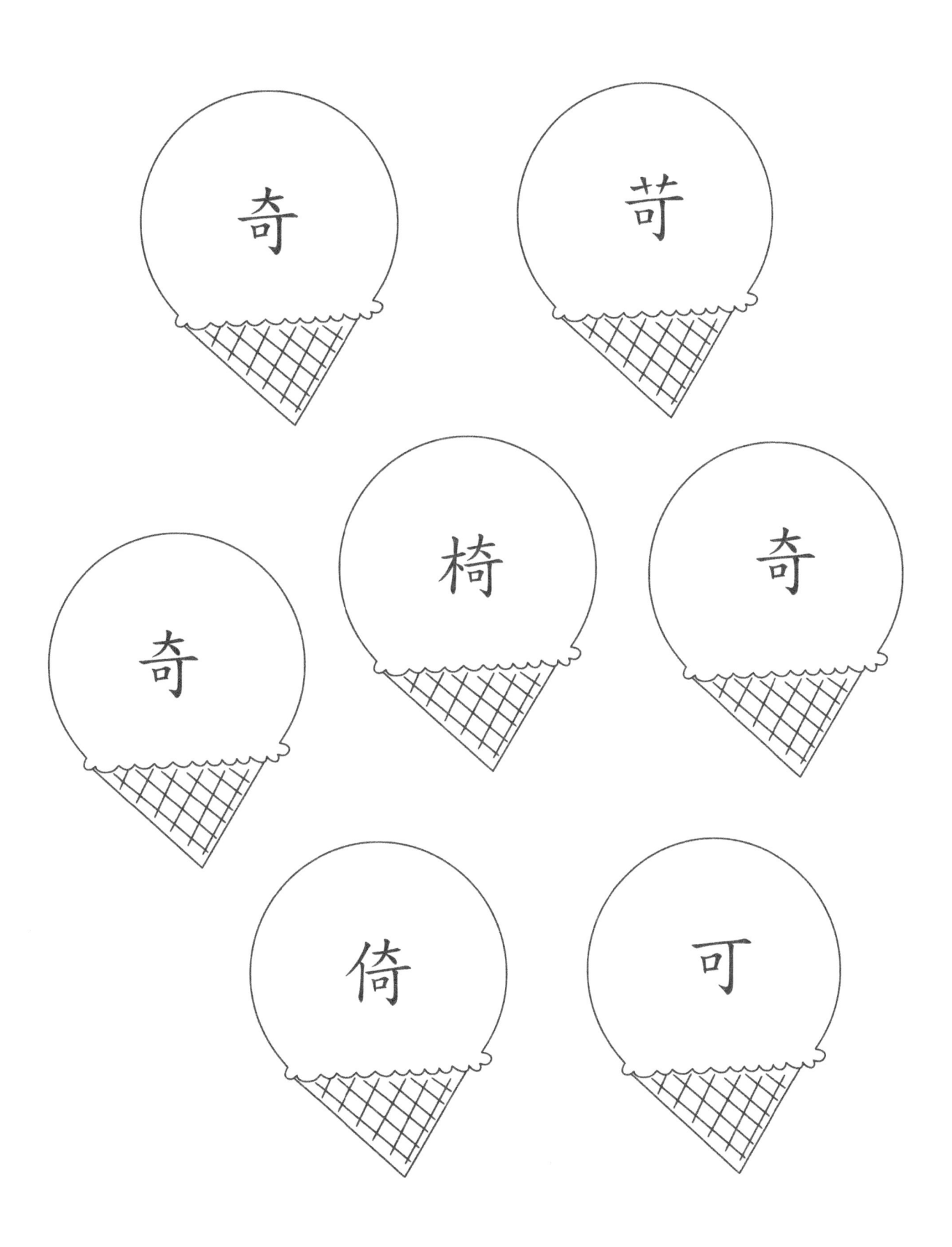

奇　苛

奇　椅　奇

倚　可

閱讀測驗。請在正確答案的前面打勾。
Read the following paragraph and answer the questions below.

這一本書裡有很多奇怪的事情和動物。小明對奇怪的東西都會很好奇，他應該會很喜歡這本書。

1. 這是一本什麼樣的書？
   （ ）有王子和公主的故事書
   （ ）好笑的書
   （ ）說奇怪事情和動物的書
2. 小明為什麼會喜歡這本書？
   （ ）對怪事和怪物好奇
   （ ）這本書很好笑
   （ ）喜歡王子和公主的故事
3. 你喜歡看這種書嗎？
   （ ）喜歡　（ ）不喜歡

唸唸看
Read-Aloud

- 老師要我們練習畫動物。
  The teacher wants us to practice drawing animals.

- 我畫了一隻土狗。
  I draw a mutt.

- 有人畫雞、有人畫羊，還有人畫了一隻耳朵很長的兔子。
  Someone draws a chicken, someone draws a sheep, and someone draws a rabbit with long ears.

- 小麗不聽老師的話，故意畫了一雙金色的布鞋。
  Lee doesn't listen to the teacher and draws a pair of golden canvas shoes on purpose.

- 你說奇怪不奇怪？
  Won't you say it is strange?

恭喜你完成了這一課，請回到第一頁將本課的吊鐘塗上顏色。
Congratulations! You have completed a lesson. Please color the bell for this lesson on page 1.

第十八課

Lesson 18 Shén – deity; soul; spirit; unusual; mysterious; lively; expressive; expression

本書中的國字筆順是依據中華民國教育部「常用國字標準字體筆順學習網」的筆劃順序彙編。
The stroke orders of the characters in this workbook follow the stroke orders provided on the "Learning Program for Stroke Order of Frequently Used Chinese Characters" website of the Ministry of Education, R.O.C. (Taiwan).

閱讀測驗。請在正確答案的前面打勾。
Read the following paragraph and answer the questions below.

每當老師說神話故事的時候小朋友們總是很用心聽。對於不知道的事情小朋友總是非常地好奇。

1. 說神話故事的人是誰？
   (　) 神
   (　) 老師
   (　) 小朋友
2. 神話故事為什麼好聽？
   (　) 因為有王子和公主
   (　) 對不知道的事有好奇心
   (　) 因為神話故事都不長

找出「神」字圈出來。
Find the characters 神 and circle them.

神　　　柛　　　神

　　　　　　伸　　　申

　　　押

　　神　　　　田

　　　　　　　　由

　　　　　　甲
　　中
　　　　　　　　　神

唸唸看
Read-Aloud

- 晚上我躺在床上做了一個神奇的夢。
  At night, I lay on the bed and had a magical dream.

- 我夢見我找不到我最喜歡的那雙布鞋。
  I dreamed I couldn't find my favorite pair of canvas shoes.

- 找著找著房子失火了。
  While searching, the house catches on fire.

- 我不但找不到鞋子也找不到出口。
  Not only couldn't I find the shoes, (I) also couldn't find the exit.

- 天快亮的時候天神帶我離開房子，並且送了我一雙新鞋。
  At almost dawn, God took me away from the house and gave me a pair of new shoes.

恭喜你完成了這一課，請回到第一頁將本課的吊鐘塗上顏色。
Congratulations! You have completed a lesson. Please color the bell for this lesson on page 1.

第十九課

Lesson 19 Hào – ordinal number; day of a month; mark; sign; business establishment; size

本書中的國字筆順是依據中華民國教育部「常用國字標準字體筆順學習網」的筆劃順序彙編。
The stroke orders of the characters in this workbook follow the stroke orders provided on the "Learning Program for Stroke Order of Frequently Used Chinese Characters" website of the Ministry of Education, R.O.C. (Taiwan).

閱讀測驗。請在正確答案的前面打勾。
Read the following paragraph and answer the questions below.

爸爸穿大號的衣服，媽媽穿的是中號，我穿小號。我們一家買了一樣的球衣，後天要一起去看球賽。

1. 誰穿中號的衣服？
   （ ）媽媽　（ ）爸爸　（ ）我
2. 文中一樣的球衣是說⋯？
   （ ）大小一樣的球衣
   （ ）同一隊的球衣
3. 為什麼要穿球衣？
   （ ）這樣才像一家人
   （ ）要一起去看球賽
   （ ）要和別人不一樣

跟著「號」字從 ➡ 到 ★ 走出迷宮。
Follow the characters 號 from the arrow to the star to exit the maze.

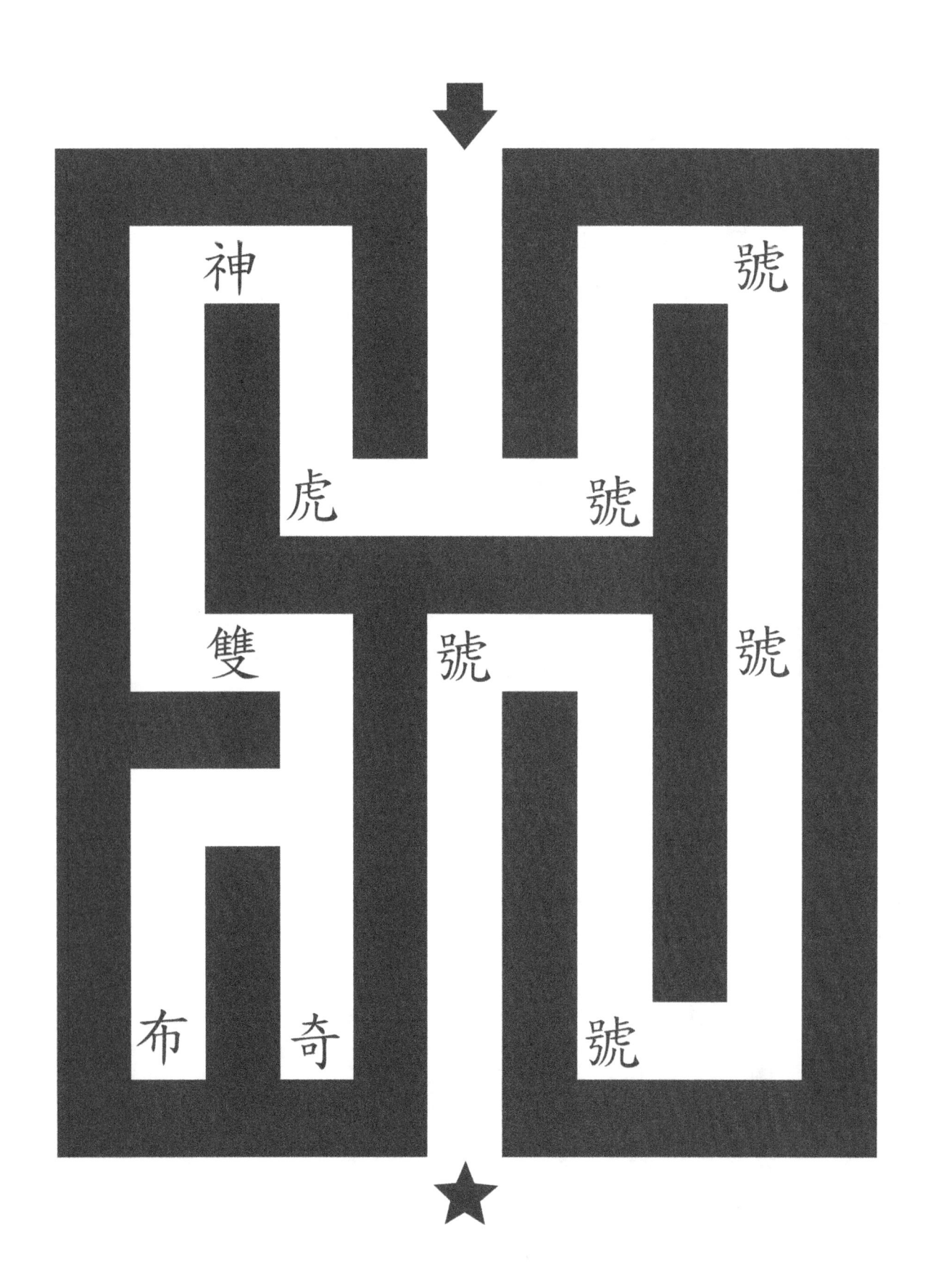

唸唸看
Read-Aloud

- 我有一雙九號的布鞋。
  I have a pair of size nine canvas shoes.

- 姐姐的男朋友也是穿九號的鞋子。
  (My) elder sister's boyfriend also wears size nine shoes.

- 我覺得很神奇。
  I think it is very magical.

- 媽媽說大人的九號和小孩的九號本來就不一樣。
  Mom says adult's size nine and children's size nine are not the same.

- 我完全不知道這是什麼意思。
  I totally do not understand what this means.

恭喜你完成了這一課,請回到第一頁將本課的吊鐘塗上顏色。
Congratulations! You have completed a lesson. Please color the bell for this lesson on page 1.

第二十課

Lesson 20 Jīng – essence; extract; vitality; energy; semen; sperm; mythical goblin spirit; highly perfected; elite

本書中的國字筆順是依據中華民國教育部「常用國字標準字體筆順學習網」的筆劃順序彙編。
The stroke orders of the characters in this workbook follow the stroke orders provided on the "Learning Program for Stroke Order of Frequently Used Chinese Characters" website of the Ministry of Education, R.O.C. (Taiwan).

圈出可以組成下面文字的部分。
Circle the parts that form the character at the bottom.

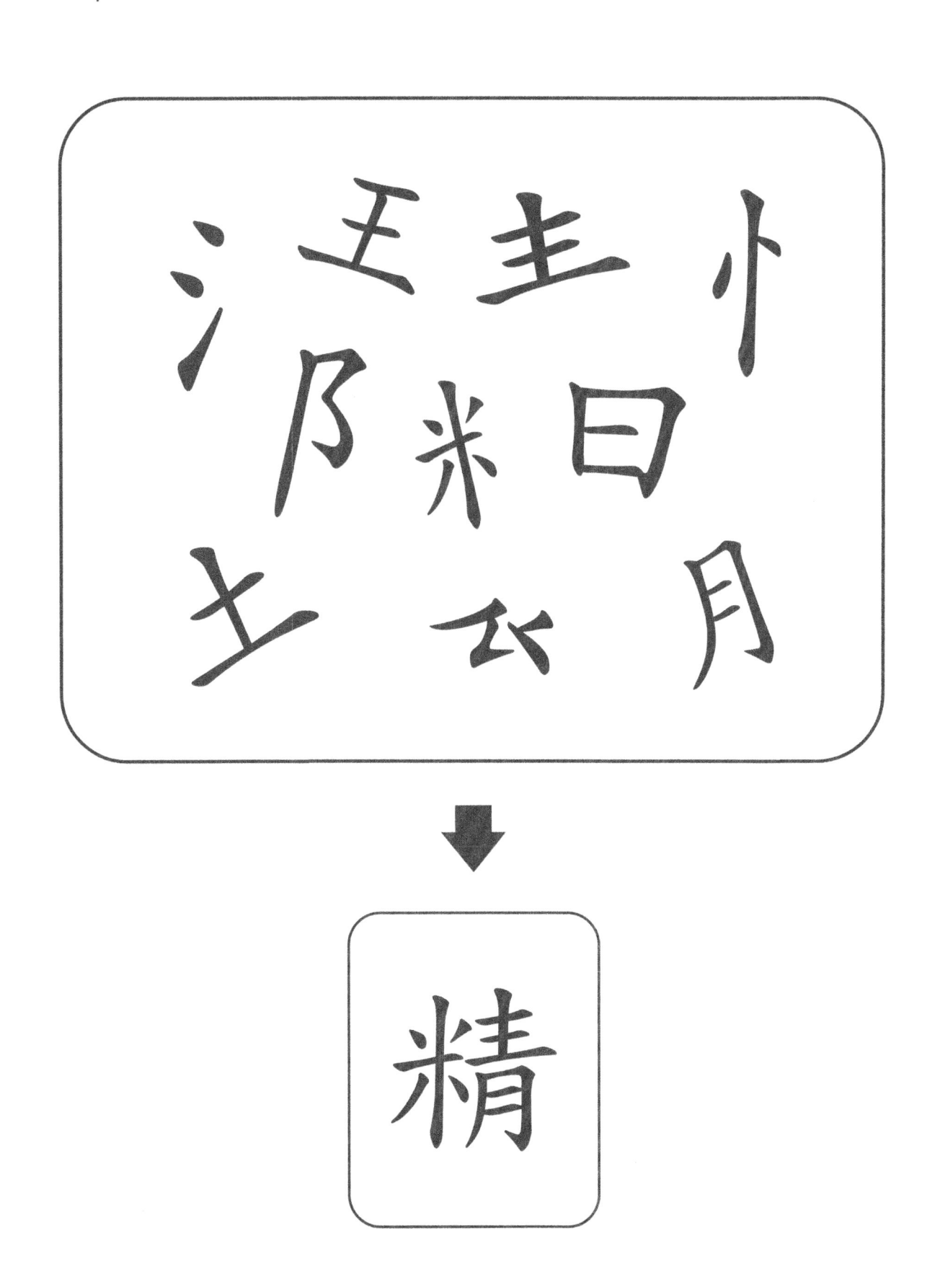

氵 王 圭 卜
阝 米 日
土 厶 月

↓

精

80

連連看一樣的字。
Draw a line to the matching character.

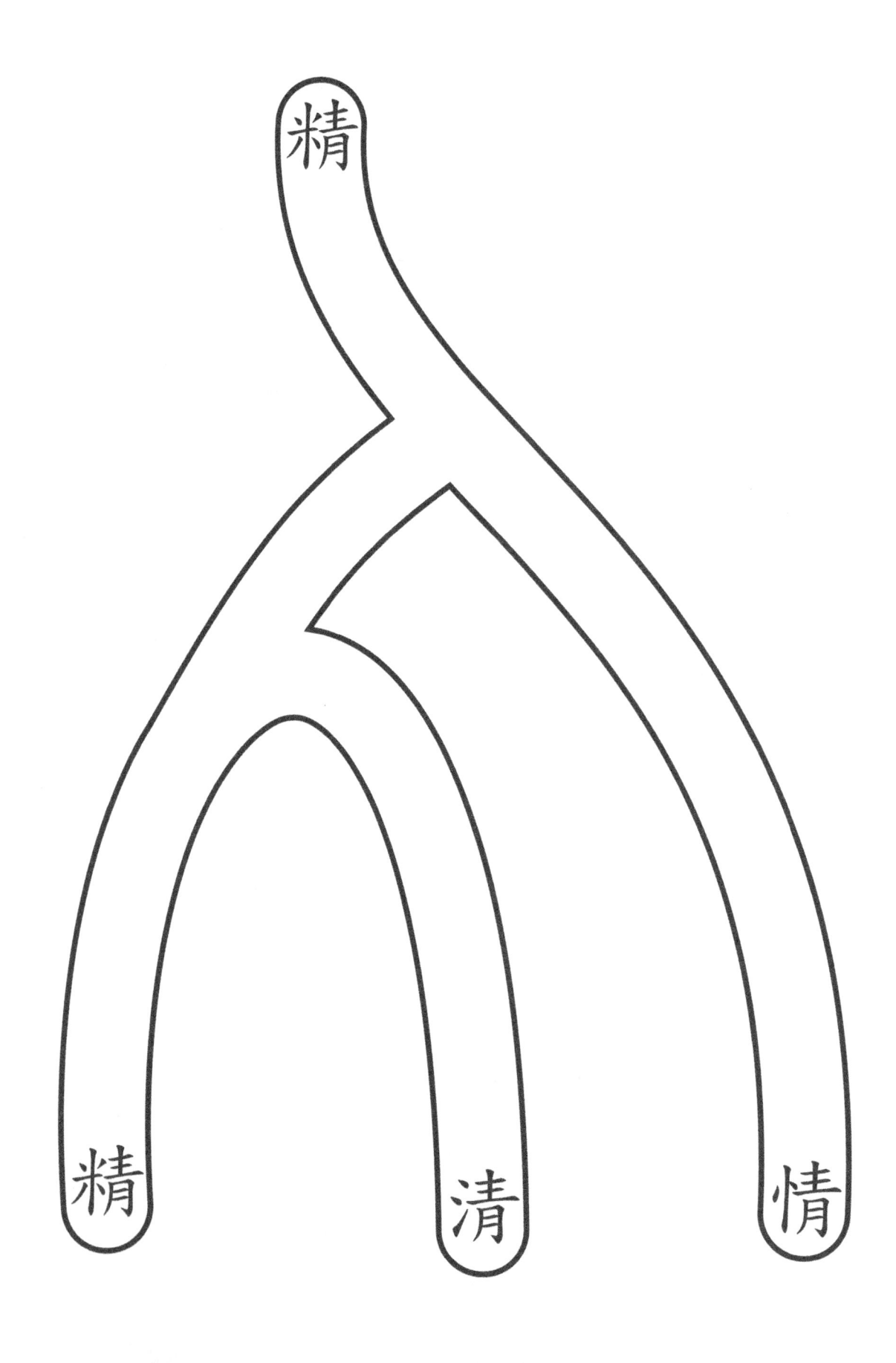

精

精　　清　　情

唸唸看
Read-Aloud

- 學校公布六月八號不用上課。
The school announces that there is no school on June 8th.

- 小奇一聽到不用上課精神就變得很好。
Chi feels energetic when he hears that there is no school.

- 那天會有客人去住小奇家。
There will be overnight guests at Chi's house that day.

- 小奇的爸爸要請客人吃飯。
Chi's dad will treat the guests to a meal.

- 小奇說他爸爸難得請客,那天一定要把飯吃個精光。
Chi says it is rare for his dad to treat people, therefore, (he) will definitely finish the meal that day.

恭喜你完成了這一課,請回到第一頁將本課的吊鐘塗上顏色。
Congratulations! You have completed a lesson. Please color the bell for this lesson on page 1.

第二十一課

Lesson 21 Yuán – former; original; primary; raw; cause; source

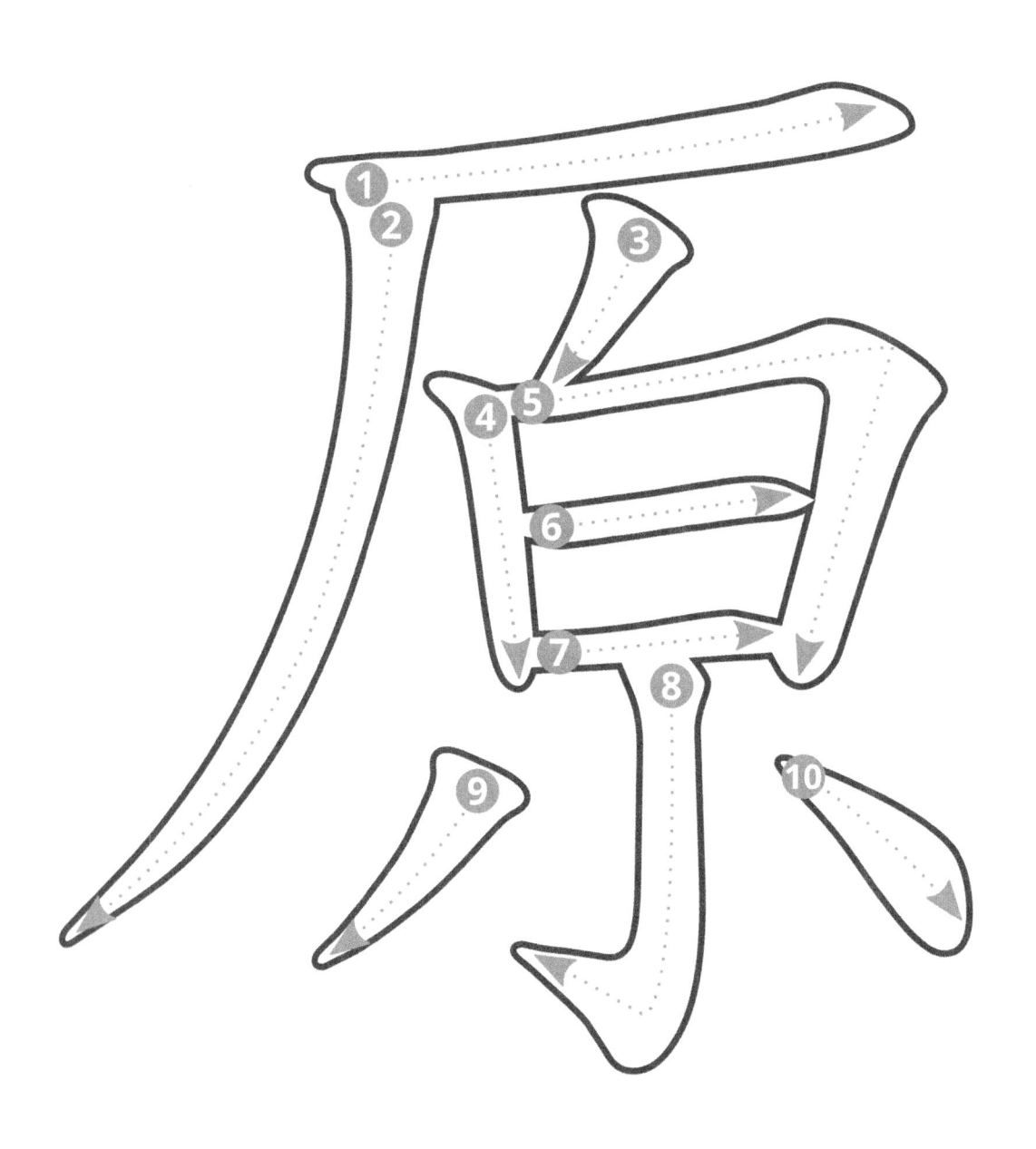

本書中的國字筆順是依據中華民國教育部「常用國字標準字體筆順學習網」的筆劃順序彙編。
The stroke orders of the characters in this workbook follow the stroke orders provided on the "Learning Program for Stroke Order of Frequently Used Chinese Characters" website of the Ministry of Education, R.O.C. (Taiwan).

找出「原」字圈出來。
Find the characters 原 and circle them.

原　　　　　　布

　　　原

米　　　　　　雙

　　　　原

奇　　　　　　習

　　百

　　　　　　原

畫出路線，連出一句話。
Connect the characters to form a sentence.

山	上	有	片	很
下	一	個	安	大
人	了	名	好	的
入	王	多	的	草
可	加	去	方	原

唸唸看
Read-Aloud

- 我跟你說一件神奇的事情。
  Let me tell you an amazing thing.

- 原來我穿得下大號的毛衣。
  I can fit in the large size sweater.

- 那件毛看起來不像是大號的,你再看一看。
  That sweater doesn't look like a large. (You) go look at it again.

- 我看錯了,原來是小號的。
  I seen it wrong. It is actually a size small.

- 你那麼精明怎麼會看錯了?
  How can you make a mistake when you are so clever?

恭喜你完成了這一課,請回到第一頁將本課的吊鐘塗上顏色。
Congratulations! You have completed a lesson. Please color the bell for this lesson on page 1.

第二十二課

Lesson 22 Tè – special; unique; especially

本書中的國字筆順是依據中華民國教育部「常用國字標準字體筆順學習網」的筆劃順序彙編。
The stroke orders of the characters in this workbook follow the stroke orders provided on the "Learning Program for Stroke Order of Frequently Used Chinese Characters" website of the Ministry of Education, R.O.C. (Taiwan).

找出到達「特」字的路。
Find the path leading to the character 特.

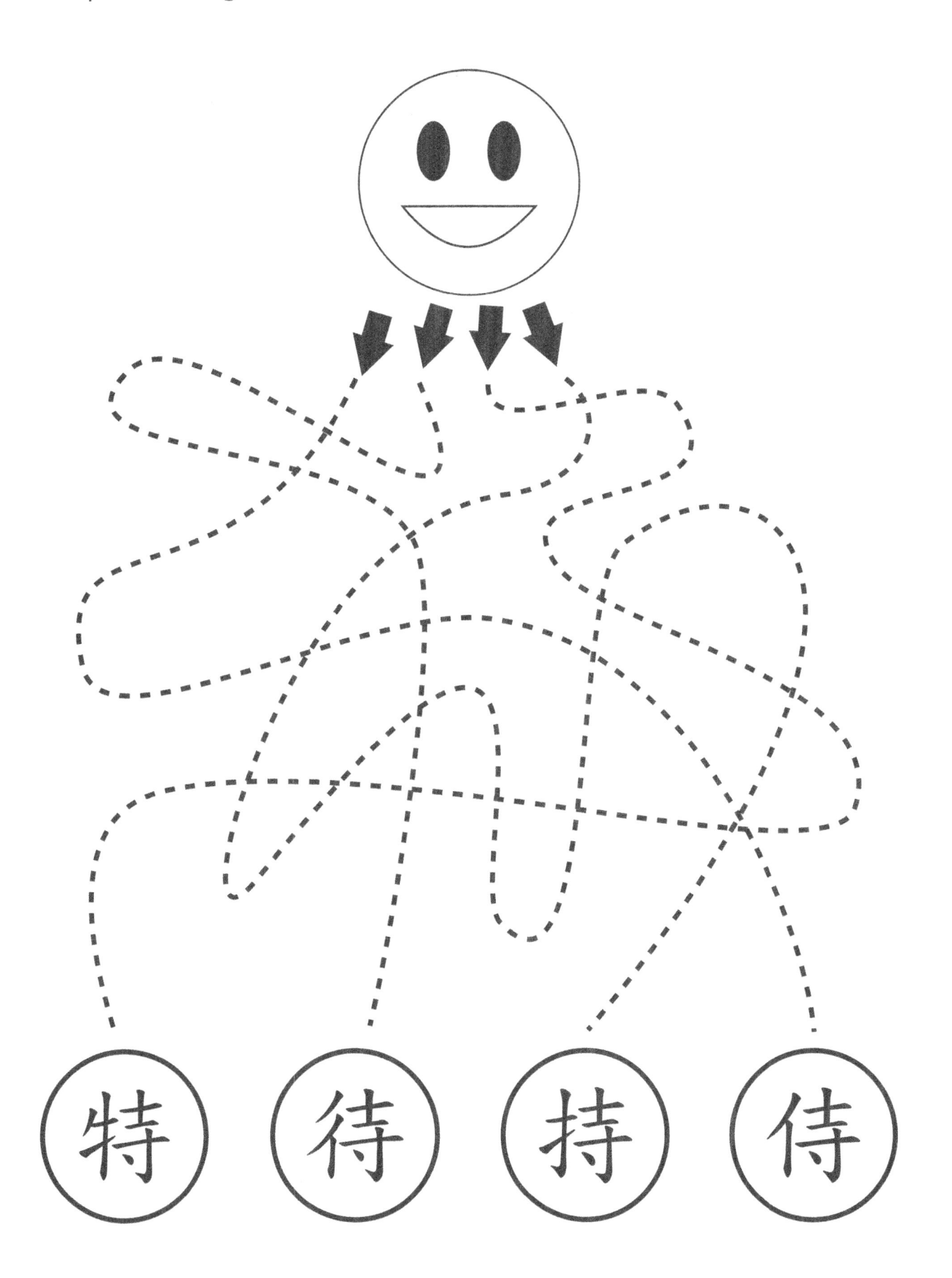

連連看
Connect the phrases to the correct pictures.

特大 •

中等 •

特小 •

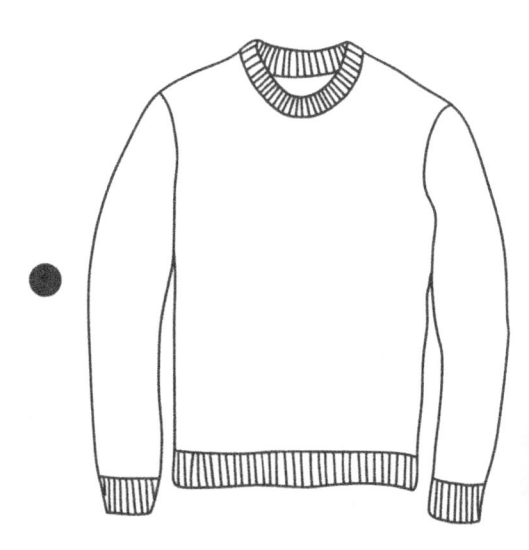

唸唸看
Read-Aloud

- 今天是七月四號，也是美國的生日。
  Today is July 4th. It is also the U.S.A.'s birthday.

- 媽媽特地包了包子讓我們帶到大草原上吃。
  Mom specially made some buns for us to bring to the big grass field to eat.

- 弟弟還帶了最喜歡的玩具去玩。
  (My) younger brother also brought a favorite toy to play with.

- 我喜歡在草原上跑。
  I like running on the field.

- 在草原上感覺精神特別好。
  Being on the field makes me feel energetic.

恭喜你完成了這一課，請回到第一頁將本課的吊鐘塗上顏色。
Congratulations! You have completed a lesson. Please color the bell for this lesson on page 1.

第二十三課

Lesson 23 Tǐ – body; form; style; system; to experience

本書中的國字筆順是依據中華民國教育部「常用國字標準字體筆順學習網」的筆劃順序彙編。
The stroke orders of the characters in this workbook follow the stroke orders provided on the "Learning Program for Stroke Order of Frequently Used Chinese Characters" website of the Ministry of Education, R.O.C. (Taiwan).

91

圈出可以組成下面文字的部分。
Circle the parts that form the character at the bottom.

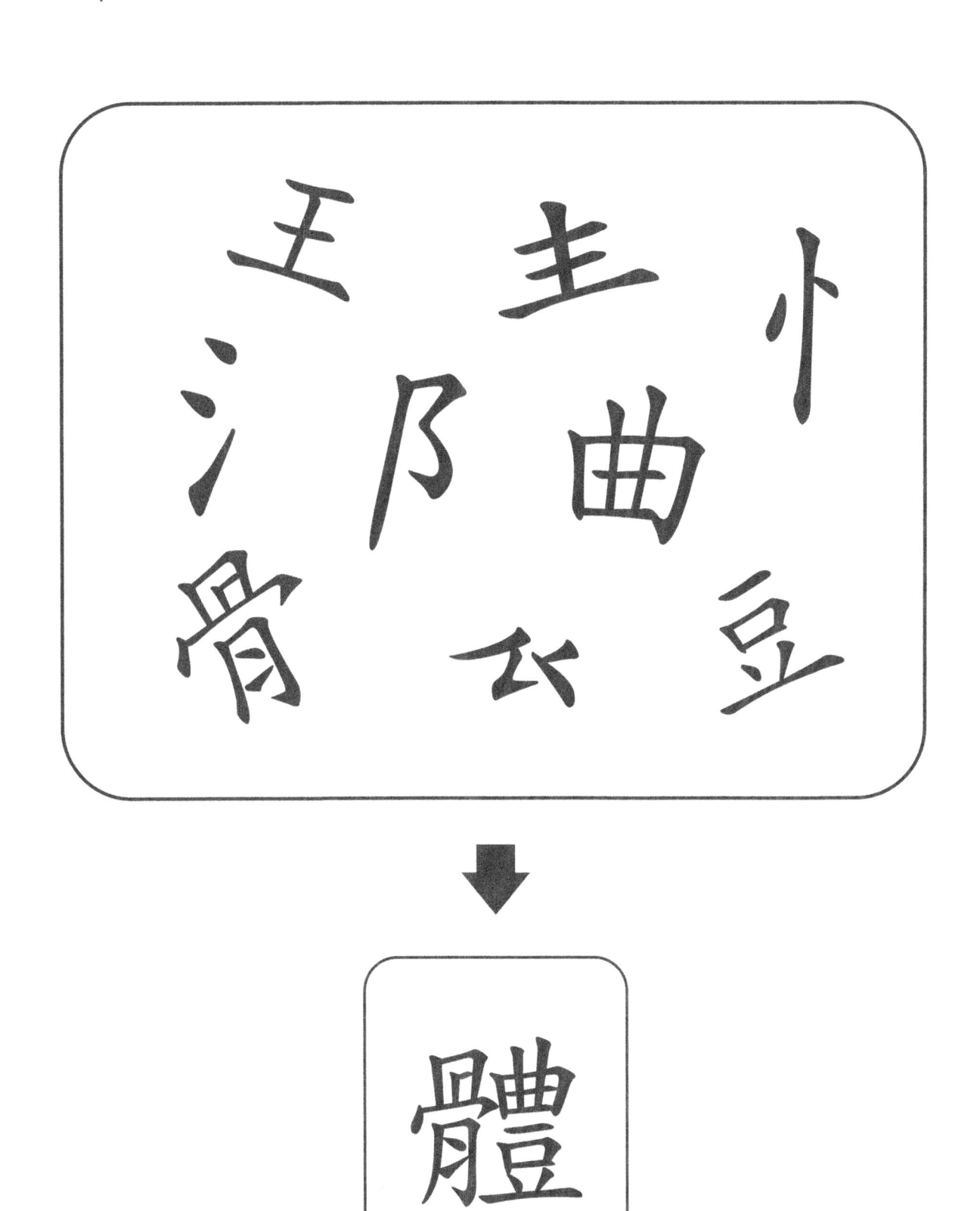

王　圭　卜
氵　阝　曲
骨　厶　豆

↓

體

請將有「體」字的地方著色。
Color the areas with the character 體.

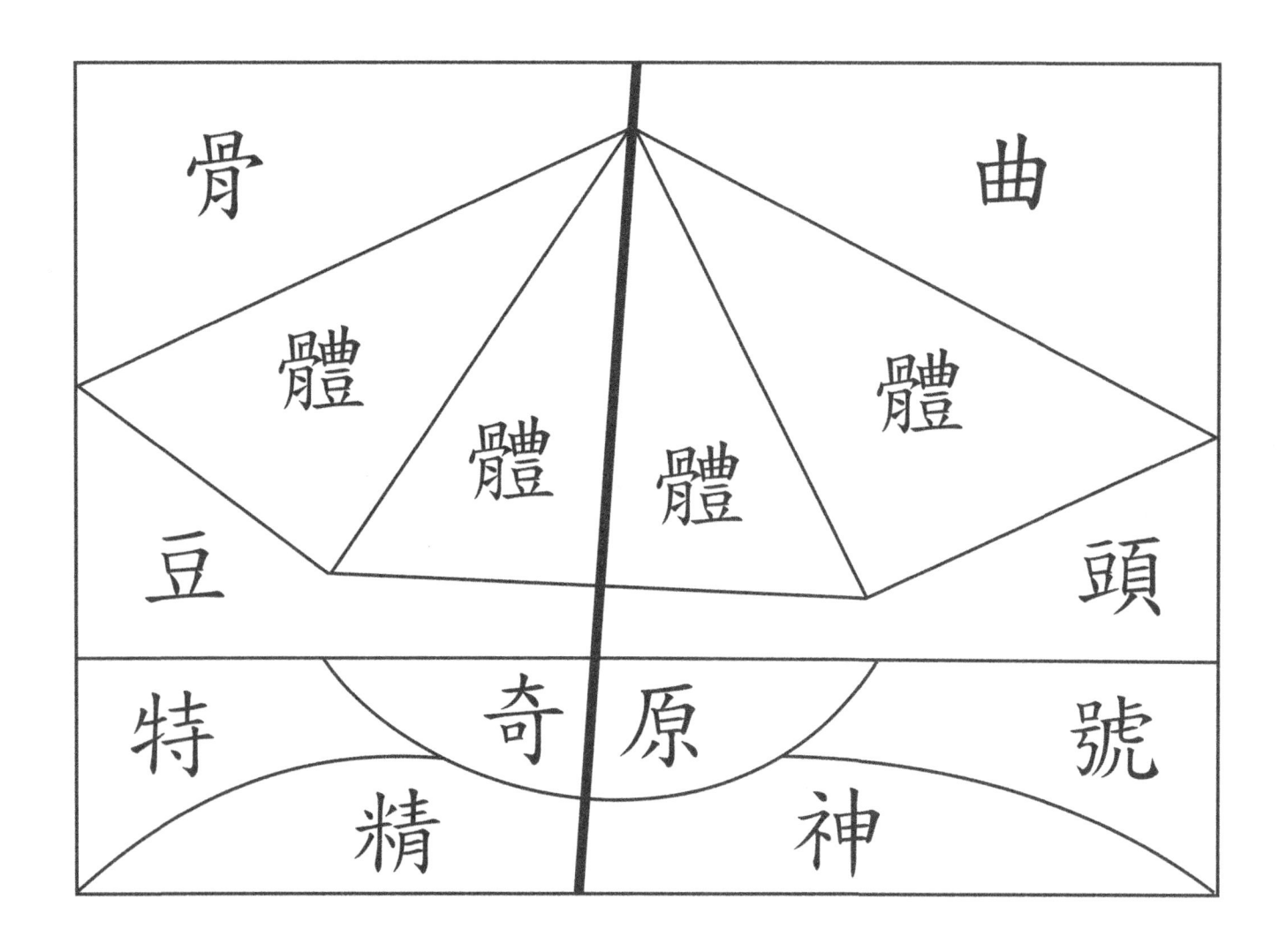

骨	體		體	曲
豆		體	體	頭
特	奇	原		號
	精		神	

唸唸看
Read-Aloud

- 他外號叫小明的原因是他特別精明。

  The reason why his nickname is Ming is because he is especially clever.

- 小王的工作要用很多體力。

  Wang's job requires a lot of physical labor.

- 他每天工作的時間很長,體力一定要很好。

  He works for a long time everyday, he must have good endurance.

- 小明不喜歡做這種工作,所以他想當作者。

  Ming doesn't like doing this kind of work, therefore, he wants to become an author.

恭喜你完成了這一課,請回到第一頁將本課的吊鐘塗上顏色。
Congratulations! You have completed a lesson. Please color the bell for this lesson on page 1.

第二十四課

Lesson 24 Shēn – body; life; oneself; personally

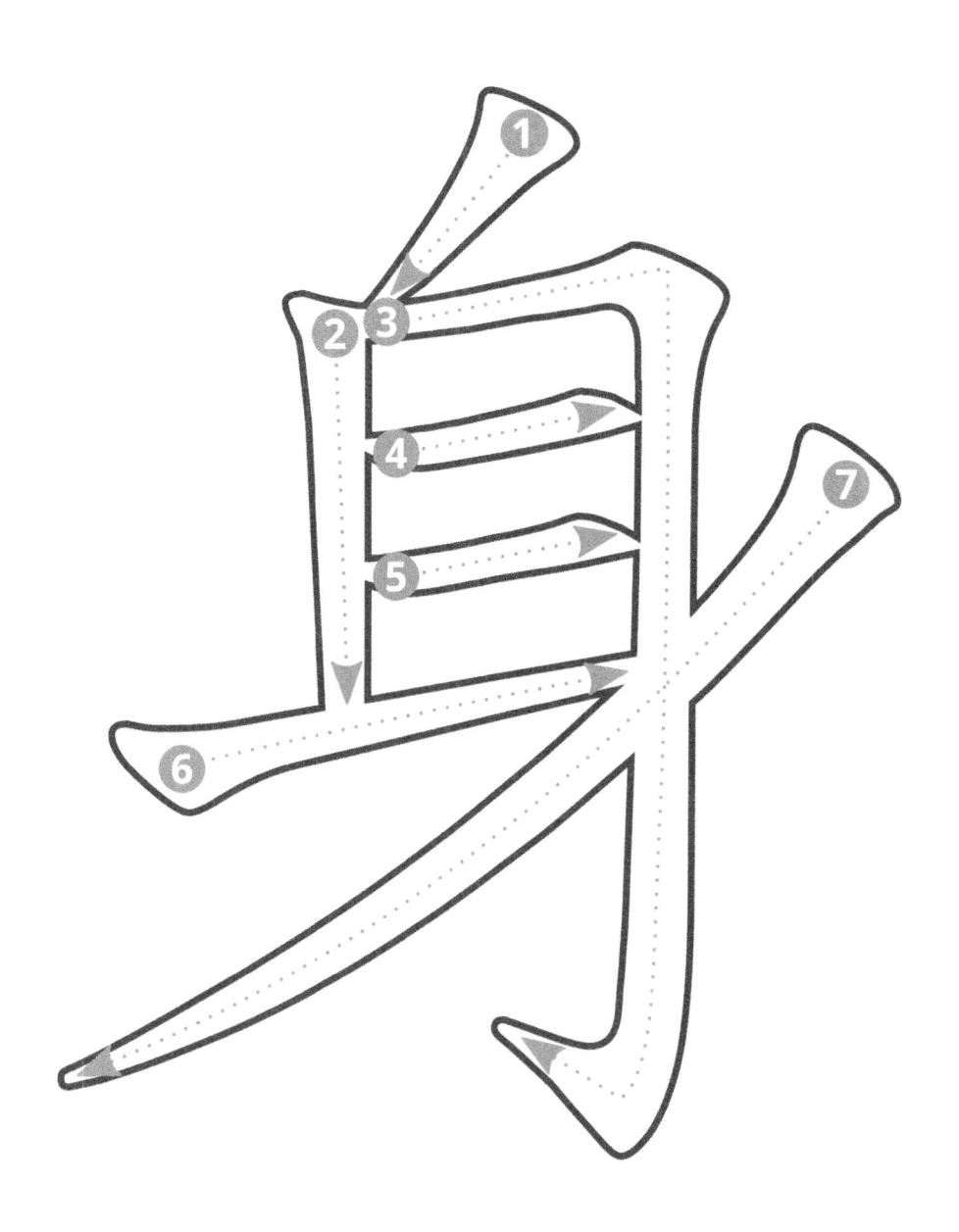

本書中的國字筆順是依據中華民國教育部「常用國字標準字體筆順學習網」的筆劃順序彙編。
The stroke orders of the characters in this workbook follow the stroke orders provided on the "Learning Program for Stroke Order of Frequently Used Chinese Characters" website of the Ministry of Education, R.O.C. (Taiwan).

95

請將下方的字格剪下來讓孩子選擇正確的位置貼上。
Please cut out the characters at the bottom and paste them to the correct location.

頭　手　身體

請在與圖案相對應的句子前面打勾。
Put a checkmark in front of the phrase that best describes the picture.

（　）小狗身上穿了件衣服
（　）小狗身上沒穿衣服
（　）這是一隻熱狗

唸唸看
Read-Aloud

- 他身體好的原因是他特別愛運動。
  The reason why he is healthy is because he especially loves to exercise.

- 他的精神也一向特別好。
  He is also always energetic.

- 他運動時都不會把手機帶在身上。
  When he exercises, he doesn't bring his cell phone with him.

- 這就是為什麼你打電話找不到他。
  This is why you can't reach him on the phone.

恭喜你完成了這一課，請回到第一頁將本課的吊鐘塗上顏色。
Congratulations! You have completed a lesson. Please color the bell for this lesson on page 1.

第二十五課

Lesson 25 Qīn – parent; related; marriage; intimate; in person; in favor of; to kiss; dear
Qìng – parents-in-law of one's offspring

本書中的國字筆順是依據中華民國教育部「常用國字標準字體筆順學習網」的筆劃順序彙編。
The stroke orders of the characters in this workbook follow the stroke orders provided on the "Learning Program for Stroke Order of Frequently Used Chinese Characters" website of the Ministry of Education, R.O.C. (Taiwan).

請連到有親屬關係的稱謂。
Please connect to the phrases that are parts of your family.

• 爸爸

• 同學

親人 •

• 媽媽

• 弟弟

• 朋友

100

圈出可以組成下面文字的部分。
Circle the parts that form the character at the bottom.

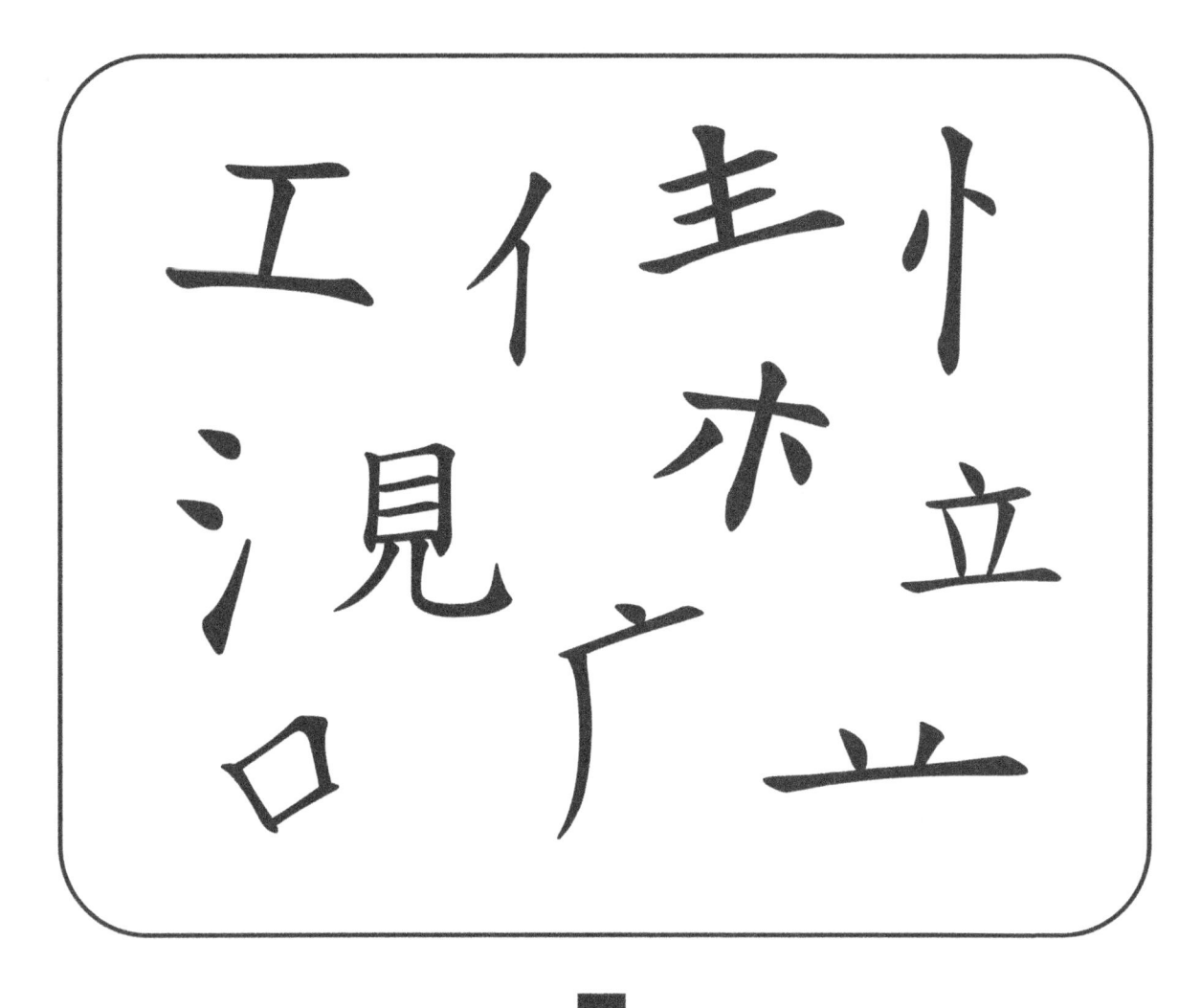

工 亻 圭 卜
氵 木 立
冫 見 广
口　　 ⺌

↓

親

唸唸看
Read-Aloud

- 我問媽媽：「為什麼要多出去走走？」
  I ask Mom, "Why do (we) need to go outside often?"

- 媽媽說：「有些事情要親身體會才會特別有感覺。」
  Mom says, "Some things you have to experience for yourself in order to know."

- 我說：「原來是這樣。」
  I say, "I see."

- 媽媽又說：「你要和弟弟相親相愛。」
  Mom says again, "You should be good to (your) younger brother."

- 我說：「好。」
  I say, "O.K."

恭喜你完成了這一課，請回到第一頁將本課的吊鐘塗上顏色。
Congratulations! You have completed a lesson. Please color the bell for this lesson on page 1.

獎狀
Certificate of Achievement

恭喜
Congratulations to

_____

完成趣味識字第十六冊。
特發此狀以資鼓勵！

for completing Fun with Chinese Workbook 16.

_____ _____
簽名 Signature   日期 Date

Made in the USA
Las Vegas, NV
01 May 2025